Copyright © 1984 Lion Publishing plc

Published by
Lion Publishing plc
Icknield Way, Tring, Herts, England
ISBN 0 85648 352 4
Lion Publishing Corporation
10885 Textile Road, Belleville, Michigan 48111, USA
ISBN 0 85648 352 4
Albatross Books
PO Box 320, Sutherland, NSW 2232, Australia
ISBN 0 86760 504 9

First edition 1984
All rights reserved

Phototypesetting by Parkway Group,
London and Abingdon

Printed and bound in Italy by
Poligrafici Calderara Spa, Bologna

HERITAGE OF FREEDOM

A LION BOOK

CONTENTS

CONTRIBUTORS

Canon James Atkinson, until lately Professor of Biblical Studies, Sheffield University, England, is now Librarian of Latimer House Centre of Theological Research, Oxford. He has written a number of books on the Reformation, the latest being *Martin Luther and the Birth of Protestantism*.

Lt Col Cyril Barnes was until recently Publicity Officer at The Salvation Army International Headquarters in London. He wrote *God's Army*.

The Rev. Michael Harper is a leader of charismatic renewal worldwide, and author of numerous books, including *Let My People Grow*.

Jeanne Hinton is a founder-leader of the Post Green Community, Dorset, England, and editor of Grassroots magazine. She has written several books, including *The Family in Transition* and *Open Family*.

Dr Charles Hummel is Director of Faculty Ministries, Inter-Varsity Christian Fellowship, USA. He has written *Fire in the Fireplace*, on the charismatic renewal.

Dr Alan Kreider is an elder in the London Mennonite Fellowship and Director of the London Mennonite Resource Centre. He has written numerous books, including one on the English Reformation, and contributed recently to *Time to Choose*, a book on the nuclear arms question.

Professor Philip McNair is Head of the Department of Italian at Birmingham University, England.

Dr Robert Norris is Executive Pastor of Program at First Presbyterian Church, Hollywood, USA.

Dr Leonore Siegele-Wenschgewitz is Director of Studies at the Evangelische Akademie, Arnoldshain, Germany. She has researched extensively on the church in the Nazi period.

Dr Arthur Skevington Wood was until recently Principal of Cliff Methodist College, Derbyshire, England. He has written extensively on Methodist subjects.

Dr Brian Stanley lectures in church history at Spurgeons College, London.

Father Simon Tugwell is Regent of Studies at Blackfriars, Oxford. He has written several books, most recently *The Way of the Preacher*.

David Wright is Senior Lecturer in Ecclesiastical History at New College, Edinburgh, Scotland.

INTRODUCTION

'All change in history, all advance, comes from the nonconformists. If there had been no trouble-makers, no Dissenters, we should still be living in caves.' Professor Taylor's judgement summarizes the theme of this book, which is an illustrated guide to radical movements in Christian history.

The twenty-one chapters cover a remarkable range of movements. What connects Francis and his friars with William Booth and his Salvation Army? Is there any conceivable link between the exuberance of today's Pentecostals and the sober austerity of the desert monks seventeen centuries before them? The thread that holds them together is that they have all acted as 'ginger groups' within the Christian church. Each movement has had something fresh and important to say, which the established church has not been fully open to hear. But in the end each distinctive message has penetrated the fabric of worldwide Christianity and made a lasting impact on the world.

Why have these movements put their stamp on the church and society, so that we remember them, while others never really broke through? This book suggests several possible answers. And a deeper knowledge of these and other movements (which space excluded) would refine those answers. But the crux is people.

Each movement has thrown up key personalities, who shaped its development. There is plenty in this book about people such as Martin Luther, John Wesley, Dietrich Bonhoeffer – all rugged nonconformists who have permanently changed the way we see things. But thousands of ordinary people threw in their lot with these groups, and this book is about them too. What was it like to be a follower of John Hus in fifteenth-century Bohemia, for example? What gave these people such joy in their beliefs and such courage in face of persecution? Where did they find the freedom to live as their consciences led them?

They would answer that it all came ultimately from believing in Jesus of Nazareth. In the words of the Shaker hymn:

It's a gift to be simple,
It's a gift to be free.

Heritage of Freedom is a celebration of that gift, in many of the different ways it has been received and experienced through the centuries.

Into the desert

Simon Tugwell

Some people think that Christian monasticism began in the sixth century with Benedict of Nursia and his *Rule of life*. But in fact it goes back far beyond that, to a time before there were monasteries, even before the 'desert fathers' of the third century. Monasticism, as a recognizable and named phenomenon in the church, has no official beginning, no official founding. It emerged, in several places at once, as a spontaneous development from the various forms of the ascetic life: the tradition of strong self-discipline which had taken shape in the church from the very beginning.

The most striking features of monasticism, the renunciation of marriage and the renunciation of wealth, go back to the New Testament. The apostle Paul recommended celibacy, in his first letter to the Corinthians, on the grounds that 'the unmarried man worries about the things of the Lord and how to please the Lord, but the married man worries about the things of the world and how to please his wife, so he is torn in two'. And this is a theme which is developed in subsequent literature. Fallen mankind is at odds with himself; one of the blessings of redemption is an inner reconciliation, and, for that matter, a reconciliation between body and soul. Redeemed people can become 'single' again. This is almost certainly one of the original meanings of the word 'monk': a monk is a 'single', undivided man, and a 'single', solitary man. A romantic notion developed too, that since we are 'married to the Lord', there is no room for any other kind of marriage. In particular, if, as Paul says, 'the body is the Lord's', it would be wrong to enter into carnal union with anyone else.

Another important strand in early Christian asceticism probably goes back to the instructions which Jesus gave to the preachers he sent out to proclaim the kingdom of God, taking no provisions for their journey as they went. By the end of the first century, at least some people seem to have been taking these instructions as covering a whole lifetime of service as

'apostles'. We hear of 'apostles' touring around, preaching the gospel, actually forbidden to stay in the same place for more than two days at a time. Their lifestyle would obviously exclude the possibility of any normal home life.

Many of the early Christians expected that Jesus Christ would return to earth in their lifetime, and this provided another reason for opting out of the ordinary practices of human society. Paul had to rebuke some of the Thessalonians for refusing to work on the grounds that they were waiting for the end. But he himself said that, because the end is near, we should either abstain from marriage or, if married, be as if we were not married.

Ready for battle

There was also, from time to time, the threat of martyrdom. Many people realized that, if it came to the crunch, a radical choice would have to be made between enjoying prosperity in this world and being faithful to Jesus Christ. So being detached from the good things of the world – even renouncing them completely – was seen as a sensible preparation for martyrdom, should the need arise. As the threat of martyrdom receded, ascetic renunciation came to be seen as a kind of substitute for martyrdom. Some people even went so far as to commit suicide as a kind of bid for 'do-it-yourself martyrdom'.

On a more down-to-earth level, some people were without the comfort of marriage through no choice of their own. From very early on the widows in the church seem to have been recognized as a class of their own, and before long they were joined by virgins who gave up their right to be married, and by celibate men too. In some places, they seem to have become a semi-official body of full-time church workers.

Practices such as these began in a straightforward way, called for by circumstances. But not surprisingly they developed a more ideological interpretation, which in turn led to new practices.

One probably very early idea was that the church is engaged in a Holy War between the forces of God and the forces of Satan, and that therefore the rules for the Holy War apply, which are laid down in Deuteronomy 20 (the newly married are excused military service). The Lord's crack troops must not be caught out like that, but must be people who are unafraid and free

Ever since Benedict of Nursia drew up his 'Rule of Life', a monk's day has involved an ordered rhythm of prayer, study and work. By living separately from ordinary society, monks and nuns show that we need not be ruled by the gods of money and success.

As they withdrew further and further from society into the deserts of Egypt, Anthony and the other 'desert fathers' were also struggling to disentangle themselves from sin. Their chief weapon was constant self-awareness.

The first monks were largely hermits, but another tradition began to form monastic communities. From these have sprung the desert monasteries which survive today in the Egyptian Coptic Church.

from the distraction of family and property, so that they can go bravely into battle. The theme of battle against demons is all-pervasive in Egyptian monasticism.

Another idea which became prevalent in monasticism for centuries was that of weeping. In the Syriac language, 'weeping' is actually a technical term for monks. This probably grew out of a Jewish practice of undertaking a life of austerity as a token of grief for the fall of the Holy City. Some Christians extended this and saw the ascetic life as a life of sorrow for the sins of the world. This could easily be narrowed down into a life of sorrow for one's own personal sins.

The habit of wandering, presumably begun at first as an apostolic necessity, acquired a new value as a sign of the belief that Christians are pilgrims and sojourners on the earth. And it could be given a sharper edge by the belief that the structures of this world, not least its financial structures, are largely controlled by the devil. So we find some ascetics rejecting civilization entirely. This seems to have combined in some circles with the belief that Jesus restores us to the conditions of the first paradise, and so some ascetics, for example, practised nudism (like·Adam) and ate only food that was naturally available, rejecting both agriculture and cooking.

Some of the resulting practices were bizarre if not dangerous. And the rejection

of the world could easily lead towards a dualistic belief – the material world as such is evil – and away from the orthodox belief, that God created a fundamentally good world. But in principle the ascetics were after something of real value. They sought a way of escaping from the domination of worldly society and the ways in which society defines what it means to be human, so that God's original plan for mankind could be rediscovered.

By the third and fourth centuries, at least some ascetics had become important focal points for a vision of humanity and even of society quite independent of conventional social, political and economic factors. Some monks in fact acquired considerable power precisely because of their position outside society. Not merely were they credited with supernatural powers (which they usually exercised in the interests of the poor, the sick and victims of injustice), but their radical independence enabled them to intervene with great authority even in public affairs of church and state. The 'holy man' became an institution to be reckoned with.

Desert fathers

Publicity, however, carries its own dangers. The pioneers of the monasticism which became the classic model for ever after, the monasticism of the Egyptian desert, seem increasingly to have moved away from the ideal of the public, wonder-working, powerful holy man. Instead they stressed humility. The wonder-working monk surrounded by his devotees came now to be seen as a typical example of vanity. And the plea of usefulness to others came to be regarded with suspicion. 'When I was young,' one monk said, 'I said to myself that I would do good. But now that I am old, I perceive that I have not one single good deed in me.'

The 'desert fathers' also rejected the ideal of wandering, and adopted the practice of simple manual work, designed to occupy the monk's time and to earn his living. Instead of the entirely uncircumscribed life of (alleged) continual prayer, they recommended a balanced life of prayer and work, with a marked emphasis on stability within the cell.

The most famous of the desert fathers is Anthony the Great, often, rather exaggeratedly, called the founding father of monasticism. He retired to the desert in about 285, inspired, according to his biographer, Athanasius, by the texts 'If you

would be perfect, go, sell all you have and come follow me', and 'Take no thought for the morrow'. The very schematic account which Athanasius gave shows how Anthony withdrew progressively further into the desert, and how he disentangled himself from evil. This evil confronted him first of all in the form of the temptation of irrelevant good works, then in the form of lust, then in the form of terrifying demonic emanations which did considerable damage to his body, and finally, helplessly, in the form of grotesque apparitions which could not harm him and which he mocked with hymns and psalms. After a long time on his own he eventually emerged again, and became a teacher. People were amazed to see that he was in perfect health of body and soul. He exhorted his disciples not to be afraid of demons, and not to imagine that virtue is difficult and alien.

In the wake of Anthony, a large number of men and some women too adopted the life of hermits in the desert. Most of them lived in settlements, with churches and priests, and they visited each other for

ENTHUSIASTS IN ASIA
David Wright

Montanus was a second-century convert to the Christian faith in ancient Phrygia (now part of central Turkey). He may previously have been a priest of the popular pagan goddess, Cybele, who was worshipped in wild excitement and raving frenzy.

In about AD 170, Montanus became the leader of a movement known as the 'New Prophecy'. (It was actually opponents who called the group 'the Phrygians', and later 'the Montanists'.) He was joined by two prophetesses, Prisca and Maximilla. Montanus was inspired by the belief that he was living in the age of the Holy Spirit. Christians should not look back nostalgically to the age of the apostles, but allow the Spirit to lead them in the present.

Montanus normally referred to the Holy Spirit as the Paraclete (the title Jesus used in John's Gospel). He was strongly influenced by Jesus' promises about the future work of the Paraclete, and sometimes claimed to be the direct mouthpiece of the Spirit, speaking in the first person, rather like the Old Testament prophets: 'I am the Father and the Son and the Paraclete'; 'I am neither angel nor envoy,

The Montanist movement began in Phrygia, in what is now Turkey, in the late second century. Its influence spread rapidly, and there is evidence of Montanist Christians in Carthage soon after – among them the great Tertullian.

advice and discussion, but in informal and unprogrammed ways.

Further south, Pachomius (who died in 346) developed a rather different kind of monasticism, organized in monastic communities, which in time produced fixed monastic rules and government. But in both forms of monasticism the major concern was with the ascetic struggle against the vices, a struggle carried on chiefly on the basis of continual self-awareness. 'Pay attention to yourself', was a favourite slogan.

By staying in their cells, resisting all distracting thoughts and refusing all religious or spiritual pretentiousness, they hoped to become aware of exactly what was going on ('discernment'), so that they could escape from the insidious wiles of the demons and from all that is contrary to the true God-given functioning of human life. Their austerities, exaggerated though some of them may seem to the modern reader, were never meant to be an end in themselves; they were meant to provide the conditions within which the monk could

---

but I, the Lord God, the Father, it is I who have come.'

But the Montanist prophets were attacked not for *what* they said, but for *how* they said it. They prophesied, it was claimed, in a manner unheard of among Christian prophets. They were 'filled with spiritual excitement and fell into a kind of trance and unnatural ecstasy'. This probably did not mean speaking in tongues, but rather prophesying in a state of intense excitement.

The burden of Montanus's message was that the end of the world was near. Maximilla predicted: 'After me there will be no more prophecy, but the End.' In order to prepare for the coming crisis, Montanus gathered his followers in the Phrygian villages of Pepuza and Tymion. They called these communities 'Jerusalem', probably because they hoped to recreate the Spirit-filled life of the first community of Christians.

The lifestyle of the Montanists was regulated according to strict standards: they were to fast often, eat only dry food and abstain from sexual intercourse, even within marriage. At the same time Montanus himself ran a well-organized scheme – far ahead of its time – for paying preachers from the gifts of Christians.

Montanus was a colourful and forceful personality, and his teaching won wide support. The New Prophecy spread – especially to Rome and North Africa, where, in Carthage, the famous theologian Tertullian became its most distinguished representative. In his view, the Paraclete summoned Christians to a much stricter way of life than before. He urged Christians never to try to escape from persecution and death.

Martyrdom was very important for the Montanists. They believed the Paraclete told Christians to hope for a death 'not in bed but in martyrdom, so that he who suffered for you may be glorified'.

A group of Christians died as martyrs at Carthage in Tertullian's time. The report of their experiences is a very moving document. It records their visions in prison and their sufferings in the amphitheatre, and presents such happenings as the promised work of the Spirit, and a sign that they were living in 'the last days': 'The more recent events should be considered the greater, being later than those of old, and this is a consequence of the extraordinary graces promised for the last stage of time. These new manifestations of power bear witness to one and the same Spirit who is still at work.' These words express the most important aspect of the New Prophecy, and strongly suggest that these martyrs were Montanists.

Tertullian wrote about a woman who was blessed with 'various gifts of revelations' and received visions and secret communications by the Spirit during the church's services of worship. She reported these afterwards, when they were all examined with the greatest care. (Women played an important role in Montanism.) But the movement was not charismatic in the modern sense. There is no mention of Spirit-baptism and no emphasis on speaking in tongues.

Montanism was soon outlawed by the mainstream church of the day. At a time when the church was settling down and developing stable patterns of leadership and order, the popularity of the prophets and their teachings were seen as threatening the growing authority of the bishops. The New Prophecy's messages appeared to be given greater importance than the writings of the apostles. Moreover, the movement was marked by extremism and fanaticism, and its intense religious excitement aroused suspicion.

Yet the condemnation of the Montanists was damaging, because no one else in the early church had such a vivid sense of the contemporary work of the Holy Spirit. Their excommunication left the church more orderly but less dynamic.

discover by experience what a real, redeemed human being is like. In particular their poverty and unprotectedness were meant to make them totally dependent on God. The most disastrous mistake, in their view, was to attempt to set up some kind of identity for themselves, some kind of life for themselves, apart from God's gift.

Although the desert fathers, at least the more articulate of them, whose words survive, showed a considerable expertise in psychology and were refreshingly down to earth ('If you see someone going to heaven by his own self-will, grab his leg and pull him down again'), they still essentially left the onus of responsibility on the individual monk.

But not everyone is capable of taking this responsibility. We find in later generations of monks much more tendency to regard it as essential for the young monk to have a spiritual father, whom he will obey and whose teaching he will follow in everything. And this process led to a blurring of the distinction between 'cenobites' (monks living in community) and the hermits. In the Greek church it became normal for a monk to begin in a monastic community and then move on to being a hermit.

Towards a rule of life

The Egyptian fathers' insistence on humility and self-knowledge meant that they played down social responsibility: – 'It is no good ruining your own house in order to build someone else's.' In Palestine,

Throughout the Middle Ages, the monasteries were the great preservers of culture, in both East and West.

Jerome (died 420) distinguished between monks and others on just this basis:- 'There are two ways of winning a fight: whether with a shield or with your feet.' Monastic life is a deliberate running away from the risks of a more involved life. Even missionary activity is shunned: 'It is a monk's business to weep, not to teach.

Not everyone accepted this. Basil of Caesarea (died 379) reformed monasticism in some parts of Asia Minor (modern Turkey) and turned it into something much more like present-day religious communities devoted to good works. And others followed suit. But this was the exception rather than the norm.

In the churches of the Western Mediterranean, there were several independent developments. Augustine of Hippo (354–430) formed his cathedral clergy into a monastic community, an example taken up later in the Canons Regular. And in Gaul there was a monastic movement, associated chiefly with Martin of Tours (died 397), which was closer to the public holy man rejected in Egypt. But fairly quickly the Egyptian model was introduced, especially by John Cassian (died 435), leading to a more secluded form of monasticism. Cassian's influence made for a monasticism more hidebound by its traditions. He was less prepared to trust individuals, whether as learners or as teachers, preferring a more impersonal 'tradition', expressed in conventional practices and doctrines.

The process of tidying up went much further with the anonymous author of The Rule of the Master in the early sixth century. His aim was to take away all initiative from his monks and to make as many decisions as possible at the outset once and for all. The monks were supervised the whole day long. It was clearly assumed that any independence allowed to them would simply be abused.

This brings us to the time of the greatly influential Benedict of Nursia. He largely followed the Master, though with a rather less suspicious attitude. He did not snoop on his monks the whole time, but was clearly concerned to regulate their life fairly thoroughly, giving them a balanced diet of prayer, manual labour and reading. His Rule is famous for its equilibrium, but, as he himself recognized, it did not make for the higher adventures of the Christian life. It was a rule for beginners, as he said, and he presumably expected people to progress beyond it as hermits, though this never in fact became normal in Benedictine circles.

The organized monasteries of the West played an important role. They were oases of Christian civilization in a world relapsing into barbarism. And they provided an opportunity for people to escape from the temptations and distractions of life in the world to concentrate on serving God. Yet undoubtedly something had been lost. The earlier monastic adventure of self-discovery, renouncing all security for the sake of the gospel had faded into the background. In its place came something more mundane: an accepted monastic definition of life, with considerable material and spiritual security.

At its best, the ordered life of a monk or nun gives serenity and freedom of spirit. Concentrating on the deepest reality of God brings wholeness to life. Monks and nuns bear witness to what is possible for us all.

The Celtic way

James Atkinson

The claim is widely made, in school textbooks and elsewhere, that Augustine brought Christianity to British shores in 597. The truth is that Augustine's Roman mission came to the court of a Christian queen, and was met by British bishops with several centuries of recorded Christian history behind them.

It was important to the British Reformers of the sixteenth century that the Church of England constituted a true part of the catholic and apostolic church, now reformed on the basis of the New Testament. The fact that Rome excommunicated the Anglicans did not mean that the British Church was no church, nor its gospel less than the gospel. There had been in existence in Britain a true church centuries before Rome stepped on these shores – a church marked by three distinctive qualities: missionary and evangelistic zeal, high scholarship, and great simplicity of life.

What is the Celtic Church?

The phrase The Celtic Church means that church which existed in the British Isles before the mission of Augustine from Rome in 596–97. Its precise historical beginnings cannot now be dated, but it was certainly founded by the end of the second and the beginning of the third century.

What are the facts? Disregarding as legendary all the delightful Irish, Welsh and British legends (of the Seventy who came to Britain, of the visit of Joseph of Arimathea and his companions, of Bran the Blessed and such tales), the first hard historical fact is the statement of Origen, the Alexandrian church father. He exultingly declared in 201 that 'places in Britain not yet reached by Romans were subjected to Christ'. Gildas, the first British historian (c500 – c570) records the death of St Alban during the Diocletian persecution (305), as does the Venerable Bede. Most historians accept this as a reliable historical statement.

The first great council of the church was the Council of Arles (314) called to take counsel in the troublous times which followed the 'Donatist' schism in North Africa. The records of the Council show that three British bishops were present: the Bishop of York, the Bishop of London and the Bishop of Lincoln, together with a priest and a deacon. There must have existed already in 314 not only a church, but a working and effective organization of the British Church to be able to organize a commission of five to travel from the north of England to the south of France to discuss a threatening schism which had originated in Africa.

Again, a Council was called at Ariminum (now Rimini) in 359 to continue the work of the Nicene Council in stating belief in the Trinity. Three British bishops attended. We further know that of all the bishops of Western Christendom who attended that Council these were the only three to avail themselves of the Emperor's offer to pay travelling expenses. No doubt this was because the British Church was poor.

In 363 we find Athanasius reckoning the British as those loyal to the Catholic Faith. Chrysostom (c347–407), the great preacher and church father of Constantinople, and Jerome (c342–420), that unsurpassed scholar and translator of the Bible, give further testimony to the soundness of the faith in Britain.

Clearly we have already in the fourth century an organized church in Britain, with its own bishops, supporting the catholic Nicene position – and this almost three centuries before the Roman missionaries set foot in Britain. There is further archaeological evidence: a Celtic church, of uncertain date, has been unearthed in the old Roman town of Silchester. It was a church of the same type as other fourth century churches in Italy, Africa and Syria. Clearly the old Romano–British Church was predominantly Celtic, and when the Roman legions withdrew in 410, the British Church remained.

The Celtic saints

During these years Christendom was strengthened by a number of great Church Fathers, biblical scholars, historians and systematic theologians. Clement, Origen and Cyril in the East; Chrysostom in Constantinople; Tertullian, Cyprian, Augustine in Africa; Irenaeus in Europe; Jerome worldwide. These men have left behind them an imperishable body of writings, preserved through controversies, wars and persecution. The British and Celtic saints, on the other hand, were distinguished as missionaries and scholars, above all by a rigorous simplicity of life of a Franciscan quality, even though more harsh and severe themselves. They have left behind them deeds rather than books, for it was to spreading the kingdom and bringing life to the church that they dedicated themselves.

First, there was Ninian (c360–c432). The son of a converted chieftain of Cumbria, he went to Rome as a young man, where he was instructed in the faith and consecrated bishop. He returned home to work for the conversion of his own people. On his return journey he was much inspired by Martin of Tours, and when he founded a church at Wigtown, he built it of stone, not wood, and dedicated it to Martin. This church, the *Candida Casa* (White House), as it was called, was the base from which Ninian and his monks worked to convert the Scots and the English. It continued for centuries as a seat of learning for the Welsh and Irish missionaries, and had enduring influence on Celtic monasticism.

During these years of Ninian's great missions there arose a British monk named Pelagius who was later active in Rome from about 383 to 410. History has classed him as a heretic, but his views occasioned a flood of fine literature from Augustine and others, and in any account of Celtic Christianity he must find a place.

Pelagius was typical of the British Church at that time: rigorously moral, highly scholarly and, if not a missionary, certainly a man with a message. To put it perhaps too simply, he taught that mankind was virtually the author of his own salvation. What troubled Pelagius was the shocking morality of the times, as the ancient Roman Empire was crumbling to ruins. He himself had a high moral integrity and believed that men and women were free, or at least had the potential, to do what was right, and were under no necessity to sin. Mankind needed only the good example of Jesus Christ to see the good and to follow it. Pelagius understood grace as the revelation of God, given in the Law and in Christ, and this work of God was meant to assist and facilitate humanity to see the good and to do it. He preached and taught his views and expounded the Bible to support them. He travelled to Africa to face the great Augustine of Hippo, and to Palestine to justify his views.

Columba travelled from Ireland to Iona, an island off the west coast of Scotland. Here he established a monastery, which soon became extremely influential, and has remained so until the present day.

He received considerable support throughout Christendom. Eventually, Augustine answered him by arguing that we are by nature in bondage to our own sin. He held a high doctrine of the free and unmerited grace and mercy of God without which mankind is lost. Jerome, with his usual abusive vulgarity, described Pelagius as 'that big fat dog of Albion', 'a great red-faced lump', 'a lout', 'too full of Scotch porridge' and the like, and took up his pen to condemn his theology. Pelagius was condemned at Ephesus in 431 and at Orange in 529.

Pelagius shattered the reputation of the British Church for simple-hearted orthodoxy, and to this day the term Pelagianism (or Semi-Pelagianism) has been used throughout Christendom to represent the man-centred, moralistic approach of self-help rather than the God-centred reliance on grace. Two bishops came over from Gaul, Germanus and Lupus, 'to uphold in Britain the belief in divine grace', men who 'took pains to keep the Roman island Catholic'. There was a debate with the British at St Albans (429), about which a contemporary historian wrote, 'On one side was divine authority, on the other was human assurance'. The great Germanus is remembered as having won the debate, though he had to return again in 447, and expel the Pelagians to the Continent where they might unlearn their misbelief.

Before the age of printing, manuscripts of the Bible were copied by hand in the monasteries. The Celtic monks developed a high skill in decorating these manuscripts, as can be seen by this page from the Lindisfarne Gospels.

Men of Ireland

Meanwhile, Palladius, a British monk, who had been responsible for the mission of Germanus to Britain, went to Ireland as a missioner. He seems to have met with little success and eventually left for Scotland. In 431, Patrick was sent to support him, and on the death of Germanus was consecrated bishop (432). A Briton, who as a boy had been taken into slavery in Ireland, he displayed mighty courage when he engineered an escape to France. There he studied deeply, and found his life's mission, namely to return to Ireland, to evangelize the land which had once so cruelly enslaved and wronged him.

Patrick was the ideal man for Ireland. He had the courage to face his former slave-master, who is said to have committed suicide at the sight of the returned Patrick. He tackled the Druids; he tackled the Royal Family. He converted several members of the royalty. Everywhere he established churches, founded religious communities, preached the gospel. By the year 444 he had founded the Cathedral Church of Armagh, which soon became the educational and administrative centre of the Irish Church.

Patrick organized the scattered communities which Palladius had left in the north, did much to convert the pagan west and brought Ireland into closer relations with the Western Church. He encouraged the study of Latin, and did much to raise the standards of scholarship. He reflected to the highest degree the qualities which were to mark the Celtic Church: high learning, a fine artistic sense, warm-hearted enthusiasm, a disciplined asceticism, and a consuming sense of mission. The life which Patrick brought to the Irish Church lives on to this day.

In the century after Patrick, Columba (c521–97), an Irish nobleman, was filled with remorse at causing a battle where many men were slain. He vowed, at the age of thirty-two, to win for Christ as many pagans as Christians whose death he had caused. Impelled by that invincible missionary zeal of the Celtic saint, he set off with twelve disciples for Iona, off the south-west coast of Scotland, where he established a monastery. This was the base for his own work, but it also proved of enormous influence not only in Christianizing Scotland and Britain but also in evangelizing as far afield as Germany, France, Italy, even Africa. There he lived for his remaining thirty-four years, evangelizing the mainland and establishing monasteries in the neighbouring islands. He out-debated the Druids, and converted the kings of the Picts and of the Scots. He outgrew his fiery Irish temper to earn the lovely name of 'the Dove' for his gentleness, and became known everywhere for his love of nature and for his love of God and man. A month after his death Augustine landed in Kent.

Columba is important to remember as a great life-bringer. He was passionate by nature, fierce in his hatred of the wrong, fierce in his love, fierce in his work and self-sacrifice for Jesus Christ. He could be vindictive, yet could burn with the tenderest love. He had compassion for the erring, and also for dumb creation and for nature. He was a man of deep spiritual insight who cast the divine fire abroad on every side 'without troubling himself about the conflagration'. When overtures were made from Gaul to persuade the Celtic Church to adopt the Roman calendar for fixing Easter, Columba in a most learned reply begged to be excused attending any such synod in Gaul. He deprecated intolerance, and rather movingly asked for 'leave to dwell silently in these woods beside the bones of his

seventeen departed brethren' and 'to pray that Gaul might find room for all of whatever race, who were on the road to the heavenly kingdom'. His tenacity could not be broken. A true Celt, he had no stomach for conferences and organization: he just wanted to get on with the task of preaching.

Here we see in miniature the striking contrast between the Celtic and the Roman type of Christianity. Irish Christianity was ascetic and monastic. The Irish knew nothing of orderly diocesan bishops; the seat of authority in Ireland was the scholarly and disciplined monastery, ruled by its abbot. Bishops were under the abbot, though in ecclesiastical rank above him. The important thing was not the rank they occupied but the work they did.

It was from this Celtic monastery in Iona that the leaders of the Northern Church in England were to come. It was by the Celtic missionaries from Iona who settled at Lindisfarne, off Northumberland, that the greater part of England was won for Christ. A long line of devoted missionaries gave themselves to the conversion of England, and the next hundred years proved to be the finest century in the long history of the Church of England.

The Irish monks were tough, ascetic, dedicated. This monastery on the island of Skellig, off the coast of western Ireland, is not exactly a soft place to live.

Invasions, and a mission

Before we examine that movement, we shall have to take note of the Anglo-Saxon invasions of Britain, beginning 449, but lasting for many centuries if we include the later invasions of the Vikings. These German tribes had hardly ever come in touch with Roman culture and civilization, nor even with Christianity. These Teutonic hordes came as invaders and carried on a war of extermination. The few remaining Celts were swept back into the mountain fastnesses. The Celts hated them and would have no dealings with them: they even refused them Christianity. The Anglo-Saxons continued their heathenism. It was a kind of nature-worship, with worship of the sun and moon. They believed in pixies, fairies and water-sprites, as well as in occult magic. It was later and indirectly, through its earlier saints, Patrick and Columba, that the great flood of missionaries from Iona and Lindisfarne was to reclaim this lost ground and win over the larger part of England to faith in Christ.

The other stream came from Rome in the person of Augustine, and though the Roman mission evangelized Essex only, in effect it came to dominate the British church owing to the powerful Romanizing tendency of Wilfrid and the authority of the Roman see. The pope made Augustine the first Archbishop of Canterbury, and, in effect, this meant the establishment of the Church of England. Plans for its organization were formulated at Rome and sent to Canterbury to be carried out. The Celtic saints had no interest in organization.

The Church in Kent grew, and though Augustine wanted to come to terms with the British bishops, his proud and prelatical manner made the native bishops dislike and suspect him. He was much the inferior of the Celtic bishops, intellectually and spiritually. There were several differences between them, such as the calculating of Easter, the shape of the tonsure, the ritual in baptism – trifling externals indeed. The great difference was that the British bishops refused to recognize any supremacy of the Bishop of Rome, and therefore Augustine's claim to be their Archbishop. Though Augustine continued to work in Essex, this estranged state of affairs persisted until his death in 604. There followed an appalling pagan reaction owing to the death of two Christian kings.

At this time, the greatest king in England, Edwin of Northumbria, had married the princess of Kent, and one of the terms for such marriage with a pagan was that she should be allowed to bring a Christian chaplain with her. She brought Paulinus to York, now a bishop. Edwin was baptized on Easter Day, 627. The heathen king of Mercia (Penda), supported by Cadwallon of Wales, attacked Edwin. On the battlefield of Hatfield, near Sheffield, in 633, Edwin's army was overthrown and Edwin himself slain. Northumbria was devastated, and for a whole year Cadwallon and his men pillaged, burned and desecrated the whole land, massacring men, women and children. Paulinus fled back to Kent. Apostasy and paganism reigned everywhere.

In a most exciting and dramatic turn of events, two surviving sons of the dead king, Oswald and Oswy, had fled north to Iona, where they received new heart and new hope, and before 'the fateful year' of pillage was over, Oswald met and defeated Cadwallon at Heavenfield in 634. A cross marks the spot on those lonely wastes, west of Hexham. The men knelt down in prayer before the battle 'having undertaken a righteous war for the salvation of our race'. Oswald was now king of Northumbria, and in his desire to restore the Christian faith his mind naturally turned to Iona, where the Celtic monks had befriended him, for the Roman Paulinus had fled the field. The first monk was a total failure, and when a monk called Aidan told the assembled monastery why the mission had been a failure, they resolved to send Aidan. Of all the fiery and effective Celtic missionaries, this was the gentlest, the sweetest and the most Christ-like. Holiness and gentleness, simplicity and sympathy, radiated from his presence. He preached the word of life, and he lived by his own teaching.

King and preacher in partnership

Aidan at once showed a love of Celtic ways as distinct from Roman when he took over office. He did not establish himself in the capital, in the ancient seat of York. The Celts never put practical and administrative convenience first. He chose Lindisfarne, that Holy Island standing off the mists of the Northumbrian coast, an exact parallel to Iona. No sacred spot in Britain compares with Holy Island. As one

This statue of Aidan is on Holy Island, Lindisfarne. Aidan chose Lindisfarne as his centre for mission to the pagans of northern England.

stands in those hallowed grounds among the silent ruins, one senses, as in Iona, the holy atmosphere for thought and prayer which inspired these Celtic saints. To the south, just visible, stood the great castle of Bamburgh, the home of his king, protector and friend.

On starting out as a bishop he neither sought nor received any sanction from Rome or Canterbury. He regarded himself as a Celtic missionary sent by his church at the request of the king. He never admitted the principle that a bishop's jurisdiction must be derived from Rome, or that a Pope had any right to appoint an English archbishop supreme over 'all the bishops of Britain'. Yet Rome acknowledged him as a canonized bishop. With Aidan began another mission to Britain.

Lindisfarne was the cradle of northern Christianity, which meant from Edinburgh as far south as the Midlands. Here was the home of Aidan and of Cuthbert, of Chad and his brother Cedd, and of Wilfrid. From here Aidan conducted his missionary journeys, a poor preacher on foot, often accompanied by King Oswald. The king supported him strongly, even helped to translate the ancient Scottish and Northumbrian speech, as well as to build of stone the minster at York and many other churches. Aidan founded a school at Lindisfarne from which the future leaders were to come. He bought slaves and trained them as future priests. On his journeys the preacher would meditate on Bible passages, or recite Psalms. He spoke to all he met: if a pagan, he would commend to them Christianity; if Christian, he would strengthen them in the faith and urge them to chastity and goodness of life. Severe on the sins and vices of the rich, he was full of charity to the poor. For seven long years, 635–642, the good King Oswald and saintly Aidan carried on a wonderful partnership, preaching the gospel, helping the poor, and founding schools.

Final rout of paganism

Disaster struck this mighty partnership of king and preacher. Penda, the pagan, who had fought Oswald's father at Hatfield (633), returned to the fight to attack Oswald. Oswald died on the field of Maserfield (Oswestry) in 642 and 'with the bones of holy men was Maserfield made white', wrote the ancient chronicler. Oswald's brother Oswy, took over Northumbria, and finally defeated and slew Penda at the battle of Winwaed, (near Leeds) in 655. He reigned, a powerful king of Northumbria until 671. With Penda fell paganism. But saintly Aidan had died in 651, and his evangelistic work was pursued by the brothers Chad and Cedd.

A young shepherd, Cuthbert by name, had a vision of Aidan's soul being carried to heaven, and leaving his sheep, immediately rode to the monastery of Melrose and craved admission. He was transferred to Ripon to help in a new foundation, but was expelled for his adherence to Celtic practices. He returned to Melrose where his physical strength and spiritual powers were such as to make him provost of the convent. After the Synod of Whitby it was he, though a Northumbrian given to the old Celtic ways, to whom was given the task, as Prior of Lindisfarne, of converting the monastery to the Roman usage. In 676 he adopted the simple and severe life of a hermit for eight years. He refused the bishopric of Hexham in 684, but allowed himself to be made Bishop of Lindisfarne the next year. His short, two-year episcopate was marked by great missionary zeal and energy, when he won all hearts by his unfailing love, his quiet patience and his manifest self-denial. In all

The remains of the abbey church at Whitby, on the north-east coast of England, built on the site of the original seventh-century church. At Whitby a synod was held to establish the unity of the English Church. Should they follow the tradition of Rome, or the Celtic way?

Further off-shore than Holy Island are the tiny Farne Islands. One of them is called Cuthbert's Island. Here the seventh-century Prior of Lindisfarne ended his days as a hermit.

this he showed himself a true Celt. Just before his death he retired again to his hermit's cell, where he died in 687. It is an ·irony of history that this Northumbrian Celt should be given the task of Romanizing the old Celtic Church. The monks treasured the saint's body, and during the Viking invasions, carried it all the way to Durham, in whose Cathedral it still rests.

With Cuthbert the epitaph of the Celtic Church may be written. The two separate streams, the Roman and the Celtic, were to meet and strive for the mastery. Oswy, Celtic to the heart, found it difficult when he was celebrating Easter to live with his Romanist queen still in the austerities of Holy Week. He wanted unity in his kingdom and called a synod to meet at Whitby in 664.

The issue was not really about tonsures and dates of Easter but the leadership in Britain of Iona or Rome. Wilfrid, though Northumbrian, had been to Rome and had returned more Roman than the Romans. The Celtic party was out-debated, when Wilfrid asked the rhetorical question, Why should the British stand out against the whole of Christendom? Had not Peter and his successors been given the keys of heaven? The king, Oswy, said that he would like to be on terms with the door-keeper when he came knocking at the door of eternity. The issue was settled for the wrong reasons.

Slowly and sadly the Celtic party walked its weary way back to Lindisfarne, whence most of them walked further on to Iona. They had asked but one thing: to be allowed to return home and end their days in the old ways. This they all did.

It has been argued that the decision of Whitby gave unity to the English Church; that it brought England into the main stream of letters, arts and general culture, centred in Rome; and that it provided the church with a consistent order. The reader must judge that for what it is worth. The decision could equally be described as the first rivet of the Roman yoke which was to gall the necks of succeeding generations for nearly a thousand years. The golden tradition of those scholarly, saintly, poor missionaries winning souls for Christ by love, was now but a glorious memory. The Romanizers at Whitby could not foresee where their decision would eventually lead – to the ultimate disaster of the Borgia popes and a secularized power-drunk papacy. It was to take a Martin Luther, and at great cost, to burn the papal bull and topple the triple tiara, and thereby show men again how right the Celtic saints were.

They were a long and steady line of scholar saints who by their missionary zeal brought life to the people of God in Britain. No one wants to return to the thatched oak shack of Ninian on Lindisfarne. But the simplicity, the self-devotion, the prayerfulness, the burning love of Christ, the faith which shone forth in those old Celtic missionaries is still the only true spiritual equipment. We might well tread where the saints have trod. We could with profit return to their ways.

Return to simplicity

Simon Tugwell

Few figures in the Western church have been so popular as Francis of Assisi (1181–1226); yet the real Francis, underneath the romances and legends, is probably almost as unknown as his contemporary, Dominic Guzman (c1170–1221). For most people, Francis is the great nature-lover who preached to the birds and who tamed wolves, and the chivalrous champion of his 'Lady Poverty'. And if Dominic is thought of at all, it is perhaps most commonly as an Inquisitor. In fact Francis really was a lover of nature and of poverty, though the heart of his message lies elsewhere. But Dominic was definitely not an Inquisitor, as the office did not even exist until some ten years after his death.

The truth about these two saints and the Orders they founded is both less glamorous and more important than the myths. Between them, they brought to the church something which was desperately needed in the early thirteenth century. Many people longed for a more straightforward, evangelical way of life. Francis and Dominic showed that it was possible to do justice to this widespread desire, while remaining within the unity of the church.

As C. S. Lewis remarked, 'There was nothing which medieval people liked better, or did better, than sorting out and tidying up'. And one of the things which they had, seemingly, sorted out and tidied up by the early thirteenth century was religious life. From the ninth century onwards the monks had been tidied up under the Rule of St Benedict, from the eleventh century onwards the orders of clergy had been tidied up under the Rule of St Augustine, and ever more effective steps were being taken to ensure that everyone who wanted to be set apart for a religious life would fit into some recognizable legal

Assisi, at the edge of the great Umbrian plain in Italy, is famous as the birthplace of Francis. He called the church of the thirteenth century to model its life more closely on the way of Jesus.

slot. Individuals seeking a way of expressing their fervour independently of the official categories were generally treated as dangerous, if not heretical. In spite of Pope Innocent III's attempts to find a place in the church for new, more simple, religious movements, the Lateran council in 1215 decreed that no new religious foundations were to be made except on the basis of an existing Rule.

Yet plainly something was lacking. A considerable number of people were disaffected with the official church, and had fallen an easy prey to separatist and heretical preachers. The generally low level of Christian education, even among the clergy, left people very vulnerable to strange doctrines. The longing for spiritual life, which held the potential for a great evangelical revival, looked like being wasted on the fringe of the church or outside the church entirely.

With the powerful backing of successive popes, particularly Innocent III and Gregory IX, Francis and Dominic were able to establish within the church official Orders which could, in different ways, cater for the demand for a style of religious life less encumbered with monastic proprieties. The attractiveness of their Orders can be seen from such statistics as we have for their early growth. We hear of there being more than 5,000 Franciscans at a General Chapter within Francis' own lifetime, and in the middle of the century there were some 1,250 Franciscans in England alone. And in 1223 there were 120 Dominicans in Paris, only six years after the foundation of the community there, while in mid-century it has been calculated that there were about 13,000 Dominicans altogether, and 20,000 by the end of the century.

Wandering preachers

The novelty of these two Orders can be seen from the reaction of more traditionally-minded churchmen. Jacques de Vitry, who was not unsympathetic, remarks that the life of the Franciscans 'seems very dangerous to me, because not only mature men, but even young, immature men, who ought to be constrained and tested for some time within the discipline of the convent, are sent out throughout the world in pairs'. And of Dominic we read: 'He used to travel round and send out his first brethren, even though he had only a few and they were indifferently educated and mostly young.

Some religious of the Cistercian Order were amazed at this, and particularly at the confident way he sent such young friars out to preach. They set themselves to watch these young men, to see if they could find fault with anything they did or said.'

For centuries monasticism had been seen as enshrining at least symbolically the perfection of the kingdom of heaven in the perfection of its structures and observances; the elaborate discipline of regular life was meant to be a protection against the frailty and blindness of individuals. The monastic enclosure separated its community from the temptations of the world. The regulated, constantly supervised, balanced, undistracted life of the cloister would, at least, keep people out of mischief, and provided a uniquely safe opportunity to grow into habits of goodness and piety. Recruits were carefully tested before being permitted to take their vow, and only mature men were allowed to adopt a more independent life, whether as hermits or as preachers.

Francis' and Dominic's friars largely abandoned all these precautions. It was the boast of the Franciscans – a boast echoed in horror by Matthew Paris, the English Benedictine chronicler – that the whole world was their cloister. And, at least at first, both Orders accepted all recruits indiscriminately, without any time of probation. As soon as they arrived they were liable to be sent out into the world.

The essential model for both Orders was Jesus wandering round with nowhere to lay his head, and the apostles sent out by him to travel round as bearers of the gospel, trusting to whatever hospitality they might find on the road. To some monks who wanted to persuade him to join their Order, a Dominican novice retorted: 'When I read that the Lord Jesus Christ was, not a white monk or a black monk, but a poor preacher, I want rather to follow in his footsteps than in those of anyone else.'

The radical and uncompromising following of Jesus Christ was almost an obsession with Francis. The crucial discovery of his own vocation occurred one day in 1208 when, at Mass, he heard the Gospel from Matthew 10, where our Lord sends out his apostles without money or provisions to preach the kingdom. Francis exclaimed, 'That's what I want!', and immediately set himself to follow the gospel literally.

He was presumably aware that many of

those who pretended to take the gospel seriously ended up victims simply to their own whims, so, once he had begun to attract followers, he went to Rome on his own initiative to seek the pope's approval for his way of life, and he volunteered a promise of obedience to the pope. But, in spite of his complete loyalty to the institutional church, he resisted all attempts to make him adopt an existing Rule. He is quoted as saying, 'My brothers! God has called me by the way of simplicity and has shown me the way of simplicity. I do not want you to name any Rule to me, not that of Augustine or that of Bernard or that of Benedict. The Lord told me that he wanted me to be a new kind of fool in the world'. Instead of the security and respectability of the monks and clergy, Francis wanted to take the risk of simply following the gospel. His Rule was not meant to be anything other than the gospel, and he argued that any dilution of it would mean a diluting of the gospel. Before he died, he tried to oblige his followers to observe the Rule exactly as it stood, without commentaries or interpretations. In his own eyes, the Lord had spoken, and all that remained was to obey him.

The literalism of Francis can be seen in his unwillingness to bind his friars to any kind of dietary laws, such as were customary in other Orders. They were to observe the fasts of the universal church, but otherwise they were to follow the gospel precept to eat whatever was set before them. He is also credited with a very literal understanding of the commandment to take no thought for the morrow: he would not even allow the cook to soak the vegetables overnight!

But the following of Jesus had, for Francis, one essential focal point. 'I, little brother Francis,' he wrote, 'want to follow the life and poverty of our most high Lord, Jesus Christ, and of his most holy mother, and to persevere in it to the end.'

Later Franciscans saw the essential poverty as renouncing property, but Francis himself saw it far more as renouncing self-will. The renunciation of property was only part of the much more drastic programme of self-renunciation. Francis wanted himself and his friars to be 'Minors', smallfry; they were to give up all the normal ways by which we protect our own interests and desires. They were to be obedient not just to their superiors, not just to one another, but to 'every human creature', and even to wild beasts. Francis himself went even further, and wanted to be obedient to everything. On one occasion the roof caught fire, and Francis picked up an old skin which he used as a blanket and walked out; later he came back and apologized for stealing the skin from brother Fire!

True happiness

Francis certainly had a lively appreciation of all God's creatures, and saw God reflected in all of them. But the key to his relationship with nature is found in his desire to be totally unprotected against anything. He wanted to take God's

The Franciscan friars lived a life of poverty themselves, to identify with the poor around them. This approach remains valid, and is practised by many Christians today as they serve the world's poor.

providence literally, as well as his words. Whatever befalls us in this world is God's gift to us, and it is a sign of self-will to take anything amiss.

The poverty of his Friars Minor is meant to put them entirely at the mercy of people and of circumstances. They are to keep out of any position which would enable them to pull strings. They are to beg for their food, or to earn it by doing casual jobs, but, Francis insists, only jobs which do not make them superior to anybody else. And because property gives you rights and so protects you against life, Francis wanted his friars to own nothing. At first, he and his companions literally had no place of their own in which to live. Soon enough they began to acquire homes of their own, but Francis was adamant that such homes must never be regarded as their private property. Anyone had the right to turn them out, and anyone who wanted to come in must be welcome, burglars being specifically included in the invitation.

This radical exposure to the chances of life, to Providence, was not just a Romantic dream. The friar, unprotected against life, must be prepared to share in the lot of Jesus Christ, who was given over into the hands of men. The way of total faith in this world is no other than the way of the cross.

Francis expressed his ideas vividly in a statement which he dictated to one of his earliest associates, brother Leo. 'What is true happiness? Suppose a messenger comes and says that all the Masters of the University of Paris have joined the Order: that is not true happiness. Suppose all the prelates from beyond the Alps, all the archbishops and bishops, have joined the Order; and the King of France and the King of England too. That is not true happiness. Suppose my brethren have gone to the unbelievers and converted them all to the faith; suppose I have such grace from God that I heal the sick and work many miracles: I tell you, true happiness is not in any of these. So what is true happiness? I am coming back from Perugia, and arrive here late at night. It is the muddy time of winter, and so cold that drops of cold water have frozen all round the edge of my tunic and keep striking my legs, making them bleed. All muddy and cold and covered with ice, I arrive at the door. After I have knocked and shouted for a long time, the brother comes and asks, "Who is it?" I reply, "Brother Francis". He says, "Go

It was not easy to translate Francis' radical discipleship into terms suitable for an organized monastic life. But Franciscans today live in a way that closely reflects the lifestyle of their founder.

away, this is no time for travelling. You shall not come in." I plead with him, but he answers, "Go away. You are an ignorant simpleton. You're not coming in here. We have quite enough good men here already, and we don't need you". Again I stand at the door and say, "For the love of God, let me come in just for this night". And he says "I won't. Go to the Croziers and ask there". I tell you, if I am patient then and not upset, that is where true happiness lies, and true virtue and the salvation of my soul.'

It was not clear to Francis or to anyone else how such a simple vision could be institutionalized in a religious Order. Francis relied more and more on other people to organize his followers, and he witnessed, with a mixture of resignation and resentment, the compromises which were necessary to save the Order from chaos. The disagreements about how the Order should develop were not the least of Francis' crosses. Broken in health, nearly blind, reverenced but also in some ways ignored by his followers, Francis received the final sign of his identification with the passion of his Lord two years before his death, when his own flesh was stamped with the marks of the crucifixion.

However difficult the legacy which they inherited from him, his followers recognized in Francis a model of the Christ-like life. Though they became increasingly settled and convent-based, and their poverty became rather a legal fiction, their boast was still that their poverty and their obedience were more stringent and more radical than those of any others devoted to the religious life. And though they became learned clerics, engaged in academic and apostolic works like many another, their essential claim was still that it was their imitation of the life of the apostles which qualified them for the job of the apostles. However muted their practice became, by comparison with that of Francis, they did not forget the dream, the foolishness maybe, of their holy founder.

Poverty and theology

Dominic was a very different kind of man, and he founded a very different kind of Order. From childhood onwards he was educated for the church, and the decisive factor in his vocation was his sensitivity to the needs of others. As a student in Spain he attracted attention by selling his much-needed books to feed the poor. As a canon

Dominic de Guzman founded an Order devoted specifically to the spiritual needs of others. This calling required a high level of theological understanding. Scholarship has therefore always been a central feature of the Dominican life.

(one of the order of clergy) at Osma, so we are told, God gave him a special grace to weep for sinners and sufferers, and he longed to imitate Jesus' self-offering by spending himself utterly in winning souls for Jesus.

At Osma he led a secluded, contemplative life. But in 1203 he accompanied his bishop, Diego of Azevedo, on a royal embassy to Northern Germany, and on the way they passed through Toulouse, one of the centres of the heretics known as 'Cuthars'. They discovered that their landlord was a heretic, so Dominic sat up all night with him and converted him to the true faith.

Two years later they made the journey again, and this time they probably met the Archbishop of Lund, Andrew Sunesen, who was planning a missionary drive along the Baltic coast. Diego apparently wanted to resign his see to join this mission, but the pope sent him back to his diocese.

On the way back from Rome, in the early spring of 1206, they chanced to meet the three Cistercian monks whom the pope had placed in charge of his preaching campaign against the heretics in the south of France. The monks were disheartened by failure, and were thinking of abandoning their

The cathedral at Albi, in south-western France, the centre of the Albigensian heresy. The Albigensians and the Cathars provided strong opposition to the Catholic church, and in countering their teaching Dominic found his true vocation as a preacher and theologian.

mission, but Diego suggested that instead they should change their tactics. The heretics were so successful because they gave the impression of being much closer than the official clergy to the simplicity and austerity of the original apostles. Orthodox Christians needed to respond in the same style. By volunteering to lead the way himself, Diego persuaded the missionaries to abandon the dignity and security which went with their official position, and to set off on foot, preaching the gospel and begging their bread from door to door, exactly as the apostles did in the beginning.

Diego could not remain there long, as he had to return to his diocese. After eighteen months of commuting between the two places, he died at the end of 1207. Other preachers came and went, but Dominic never looked back.

This was the beginning of Dominic's true vocation as a preacher, and, after he had attracted a few followers who were prepared to commit themselves to him, he was able to found his Order of Preachers, first as a diocesan institute in Toulouse, then, in 1216, as an international Order recognized by the pope. To satisfy the requirements of the Lateran Council he and his brethren had to adopt an existing Rule and, not surprisingly, they opted for the Rule of St Augustine, the Rule of the 'canons', or clergy; but the preaching friars were nonetheless a very different kind of Order from the canons.

The highest value in their life was given to the spiritual need of others. The Order was officially declared to exist specifically 'to be useful to the souls of our neighbours'. The traditional monastic observances which the friars retained took second place to their mission in the world. Within their communities they extended in an unprecedented way the principle of 'dispensation' – special permission to break the Rule for particular reasons. Dispensations were no longer unavoidable concessions to individual weaknesses, but a concession to the job which the Order had to do. The routine of the convent must never be allowed to interfere with preaching or with that life of study which necessarily went along with it. And, of course, many of the friars spent a considerable amount of time outside their convents, wandering round in pairs, preaching.

From the point of view of traditional monasticism, the Dominicans were taking an enormous risk, in exposing themselves like this to the temptations and distractions of the world. But the job was too urgent to wait until the friars felt themselves to be secure. Monastic prudence and even, to some extent, intellectual and spiritual training, were replaced by an immense confidence in God.

Just as the first preachers of the gospel went forth in the power of the Holy Spirit, prepared to be dependent on God for their inspiration and everyday support, so the Dominican friars went out, trusting that God would give them the words to say, and not wasting time securing their own financial backing. They were beggars in a double sense: they begged their temporal sustenance from the people among whom they worked, and they begged their spiritual sustenance from God, relying on him to provide both the grace to make them effective preachers and whatever they needed for their own salvation. The fifth Master of the Order, Humbert of Romans, one of the greatest exponents of Dominican life in the thirteenth century, is quite explicit about the risk that the preachers take. He even talks, echoing the Cistercian Bernard of Clairvaux, of 'the sins which will unavoidably occur' in the course of their active life of service. A busy preacher cannot expect to have the efficient, immaculate spiritual life of a monk! But preachers are God's feet and if they get dirty – and they will get dirty – the generosity of their service will wash the dirt off again. The job is risk and remedy in one.

The only totally essential discipline was study. The most necessary mission was to teach the faith, and so the friars had to know their theology. Dominic had learned this very early on in his mission. After one debate with the heretics, during the lifetime of Diego, one of the people present commented, 'Who would have thought that the Catholics had so many arguments on their side?' The enemy was ignorance, more than ill-will. So, as soon as Dominic had established his little community in Toulouse, he started taking them to theology lectures, and shortly after that he sent some of them to Paris to attend the University. In later decades the Order made a special point of moving into university centres. When the friars came to England in 1221, they went straight to Oxford to make their first foundation there.

The other primary observance was poverty. Dominic, like Diego, appreciated that the job of the apostles called for the lifestyle of the apostles. But, although Dominic himself was as enthusiastic for extreme poverty as Francis was, the Order was always clear that poverty, for the Dominicans, was a means not an end. They adapted their economy as they went along, and in the course of the centuries they had to abandon their original total dependence on soliciting gifts, because it was interfering with their work.

The essential poverty was not so much financial as personal. The Dominicans took the risk of throwing themselves totally into the work of God, identifying themselves with a grace which God might want to give to others through them, rather than seeking grace for themselves. They took the risk of endangering their own orderly spiritual growth, their own contemplative tranquillity, their own life of prayer, everything, in order to be the bearers of God's word in the world. They accepted the challenge of the new intellectual movements of the time, at the risk of being considered dangerous innovators, in order to save people's minds for Jesus.

Inevitably, as their numbers increased, the life of the convent became more important. They could not all be preaching all the time, and they were not all gifted for a serious intellectual life. And the policy of drawing recruits from the whole wide world evidently filled their convents with what some people called 'useless young men', who then had to be subjected to more rigorous discipline. And inevitably, over the ages, their apostolic and intellectual fervour waxed and waned. But the ideal of following Jesus the preacher remained alive, and has shown itself resilient to our own times.

Protest and renewal

Alan Kreider

'They go about two by two, barefoot, clad in woollen garments, owning nothing, holding all things common like the apostles, naked, following a naked Christ. They are making their first moves now in the humblest manner because they cannot launch an attack. If we admit them, we shall be driven out.'

So wrote twelfth-century churchman Walter Map in response to the early Waldensians. His words illustrate how eager were the late medieval 'heretics' to experience in their own time the vitality of the earliest Christians. They show too that members of the medieval religious establishment could feel severely threatened by attempts radically to renew the church.

In the late Middle Ages there were three major movements which shared that goal: the Waldensians, the Lollards and the Czech Brethren. These movements differed in various ways, but they had significant similarities. Each of them reacted against a church which through wealth, privilege and power had moved far from the teachings of Jesus and the dynamic simplicity of the early Christians. Each of them emphasized preaching from a Bible in the language of the people. Each of them owed its strength to the dedicated involvement of laymen and laywomen. And despite the fact that in every case the church responded by Inquisition and burning, each of these movements survived into the sixteenth century to encounter the Reformation.

The Waldensians were first on the scene. This movement began in the 1170s with the conversion of a prominent merchant from Lyons named Valdes. (His precise dates are unknown but he died before 1218). Valdes was moved by a minstrel's recounting of the story of St Alexis, who had left his patrician Roman parents to live a life of apostolic poverty. He went for counsel to a theologian, who shared with him Jesus' words to the rich young man: 'If you want to be perfect, go sell what you have.' Having made provision for his wife and daughters, Valdes – like Zacchaeus, the

tax collector in the Gospel story – made restitution to those from whom he had made unjust profits. He commissioned two priests to translate major portions of the Bible and the Church Fathers from Latin into the Provençal dialect, and then proceeded to study and memorize these. Joyfully he gave to the poor all his remaining property, and began to travel on foot. His watchword was, 'No man can serve two masters!'

From the outset people warmed to Valdes' attractive preaching and lifestyle. Soon some of them, both men and women, were leaving their security and joining him. Their commitment was to spread the gospel in their native tongue, to identify with the poor by becoming poor themselves, and to take the teachings of Jesus – which had often been viewed as optional advice for the holy or eccentrics – as the rule of life for all Christians.

Valdes' hope was that the preaching and example of his itinerant followers (the 'Poor in Spirit') would be a spur to the renewal of the whole church. At first some churchmen, including Pope Alexander III, gave them cautious encouragement. But within a decade the bishops had forbidden them to preach. They persisted, quoting Peter and John's words in Acts: 'We must obey God rather than men' . And so they were banished from Lyons. For the next 300 years they were to be on the run, at times persecuted severely.

Nevertheless, the movement spread. Inspired by the story of Jesus commissioning the Twelve, Waldensian evangelists preached throughout southern France and established a network of sympathizers extending as far north as Alsace and the Netherlands. They also found a ready audience in northern Italy, where for some time already dissident religious groups had been gaining strength. The Italian Waldensians (the 'Poor Lombards') soon asserted independence of their French brothers (the 'Poor Lyonists'), for they were developing distinctive features of their own. Their concern was not only to travel and preach. They worked to nurture the ordered life of Christian community, based on the early chapters of the Acts of the Apostles. Their style was more organized and less spontaneous than their French brothers and sisters. But the Italians also evangelized. By 1211 their community in Strasbourg was strong enough spiritually and numerically to produce eighty martyrs.

And soon there were other Waldensian communities of the Italian connection as far north-east as Moravia and as far south as the heel of Italy.

The dangerous Bible

During the thirteenth century the church, through the newly-founded Inquisition, did its best to snuff out the Waldensian movement. The fear of the churchmen was transparent and, from their point of view, well-grounded. For the Bible is a dangerous book. In the hands of the 'stupid and uneducated' it can be subversive. Hence the churchmen preferred to keep it in a learned tongue, Latin, for the use of privileged intellectuals.

The Waldensian translations opened the Bible to laypeople, for whom it became the final authority for belief and life: 'Whatever a doctor of the church teaches that he cannot prove by the text of the New Testament, they consider to be a complete fable.'

To their critics, their interpretations seemed unduly literal. The Waldensians

The Waldensians spread far and wide in continental Europe. But as they were persecuted their life began to centre on inaccessible places, often high mountain valleys.

believed that Jesus had meant what he had said when he told his disciples not to swear oaths or to accumulate treasure on earth. He had likewise expected his disciples obediently to sheathe their swords and to love their enemies. According to the New Testament, the apostles and the early Christians had been faithful to his teaching. Not so, the Waldensians were convinced, the churchmen of their own day: 'The apostles did not live this way, nor do we, who are imitators of the apostles.' This negative comparison was a potent corrosive for dissolving the legitimacy of the established church.

At first the Waldensians did not want to displace the church. They simply wanted to supply what was lacking in it – obedience to Jesus, authentic community, and 'the voice of the gospel'. But as its resistance to change stiffened and its persecuting zeal intensified, the Waldensians were forced either to accommodate themselves to the church or, at the risk of burning, to get out.

In the early thirteenth century many chose the former course, some even forming what was almost a monastic order, the 'Catholic Poor'. Yet others chose to leave the church. It had been seduced by power, they came to believe, since the time of the emperor Constantine; it was 'infused with the venom of temporal wealth.' Thereby it had departed from the apostolic heritage. So, although many Waldensians made public appearance in services in their parish churches, they found their true fellowship and nurture in illicit cells of brothers and sisters.

These Waldensian cells, meeting generally at night, in houses and barns, were marked by intense activity. Those present were laypeople, often 'persons of basest occupations' such as tailors, shoemakers and smiths. Women were there in disproportionate strength. Largely excluded from using their gifts in the church, they were finding among the 'heretics' liberty to teach and preach. Everyone participated: 'Old and young, men and women, by day and by night, they do not stop their learning and teaching others.' Illiterates were learning to read: 'Learn but one word a day,' they admonished each other, 'and after a year you will know three hundred, and then you will progress.' The Bible was memorized and recited. In Austria one critic found an 'unlearned rustic who could recite the Book of Job word for word, and many others who know the entire New Testament perfectly'. After recitations, the Bible would be commented upon and applied. Many of these applications were anticlerical; and Waldensians had little tolerance for medieval beliefs and practices such as relics, holy days and purgatory. They were especially suspicious of sacraments administered by priests of dubious morals.

The Waldensians translated the Bible into the common languages, and laid great stress on teaching it and learning from it together. They believed that it taught the way of true freedom.

Before long the Waldensians began to develop a leadership structure of their own. At the behest of a *rector* (bishop), *majores* (presbyters) and *minores* (deacons) travelled from one Waldensian cell to another, preaching and hearing confessions. On Maundy Thursday, when cells met to celebrate the Lord's Supper, the believers often washed each other's feet, after which the itinerant minister distributed the elements of bread, wine and fish.

The Lollards

By the late fourteenth century, the Waldensian movement was losing momentum. Persecution was finally beginning to be effective, not only in burning Waldensians or forcing them to recant, but also in causing them to become introverted and to lose their evangelistic zeal. Geographically the communities clustered in mountainous areas – especially the Cottonian Alps – where they were more secure. And two other movements arose to take over from the flagging Waldensians the task of challenging medieval Christendom.

One of these, the Lollards, came to resemble the Waldensians in many ways, even though it developed quite independently. They got their name from a Middle Dutch insult meaning 'mumbler' of prayers, and they were adherents of an English movement which was the offspring of a brilliant Oxford don, John Wyclif (died 1384). It was not Wyclif's charisma which launched the movement; it was his ideas.

Wyclif was a mature convert to 'realism' in philosophy and to Augustine's theology. As these ideas germinated in his mind, their practical implications became clear, and he set these forth with undiplomatic boldness.

The Bible, he was convinced, had been conceived in God's mind before creation. It was therefore entirely true, and the exclusive criterion of faith and practice, far superior to church tradition. Everyone ought to have access to its truth in his own language: 'No man is so rude a scholar but that he may learn the words of the gospel according to his simplicity.' The church likewise was an ideal reality, predestined by God to be the body of the elect. Thus both the Bible and the true church stood in judgement upon the actual church, which Wyclif increasingly came to see as a 'synagogue of Satan'. It had departed from

John Wyclif opposed many of the tendencies of the fourteenth-century church. His teaching helped prepare the way for the Reformation. His followers, the Lollards, believed that God would 'reform our church, as being entirely out of joint, to the perfectness of its first beginning'.

the purity of its early poverty; it had lost its authority to interpret the Bible; and it had become entangled in a great web of abuse. Pilgrimage, purgatory, transubstantiation, along with many other aspects of ecclesiastical life, came under Wyclif's searing attack. Only the king, he was convinced, as God's true vicar could intervene to reform the hopelessly compromised church.

At first Wyclif had many politically influential supporters. But his ideas, especially on the 'eucharist', or holy communion, soon developed to a point where he alienated many of them. In 1382 the church authorities were able to purge him and his followers from Oxford. And in the next two decades, despite attempts by 'Lollard knights' and other sympathizers to secure reform by parliamentary means, the repression of the movement proceeded. A rebellion led by Sir John Oldcastle in 1414 was a desperate expression of frustration, and its easy suppression by Henry V marked the end of the Lollard attempt to reform the church from above.

From the outset, however, there had been many Lollards who had sought renewal from below, through preaching rather than politics. Wyclif had equipped his university-trained followers with an arsenal of arguments. And soon they had both popularized these arguments in a series of tracts and sought to justify them by the Bible, which they twice translated into English. Preachers criss-crossed England and Wales carrying Wyclif's ideas in simplified form. And even after persecution had removed the first-generation evangelists from circulation, less educated preachers arose to take their place. Despite successive waves of persecution, the Lollard movement survived in many places, as cells of believers continued to gather.

The life of the Lollards

The Lollard cells did not, so far as we know, administer the sacraments. For that they would attend their parish churches, even though they might give indication of their disaffection by 'sitting mum like beasts' at the elevation of the Host. Nor do these cells seem to have had membership rolls. Attending their meetings in 'nooks and corners', houses and barns, were friends who knew that they could trust each other. These 'known men' and women were links in a chain of inspiration and support joining one Lollard community with another.

Not surprisingly they tended to intermarry. They were served by roving booksellers and evangelists, one of whom with his wife 'had turned six or seven hundred people unto those opinions'. A few priests participated in the movement, as did some wealthy urban merchants. But predominantly the Lollards were laypeople, especially those in the cloth trade. As with the Waldensians, women were prominent in the movement, reciting and expounding the Bible. One woman exulted – probably accurately enough – that she was as learned as her priest, except in the mass.

The central activity of these cells was reading the English Bible. One group in Buckinghamshire asked a boy whom they were not sure they could trust to leave them 'that he should not hear and tell'. Then the leader 'did recite certain places to them out of the Epistles of St Paul, and of the Gospels'. These Scriptures were of course available only in manuscript, and so expensive to buy; like other English books, they were also dangerous to possess. So, although some people had good collections ('book of Luke and one of Paul, and a gloss of the Apocalypse'), many others could possess the Bible only by memorizing it. Groups of believers stayed up all night to do this. Some of them took private instruction to commit the Beatitudes to heart. Whenever the Lollards in Burford met, they called upon a woman who çould declaim in English 'the declaration of the Ten Commandments, and the Epistles of Peter and James'.

From the Bible the Lollards obtained fuel for their anticlericalism, which at times

A statue of John Hus, in the village of Husinec where he was born. Hus still holds great interest for the people of Czechoslovakia, because he presented a radical challenge to the church establishment of his time.

they expressed quite rudely. They could find no warrant in the Bible for pilgrimages or images, which they viewed as idols. Nor did they have much patience with priestly or saintly mediators.

'What need is it,' one woman asked, 'to go to the feet, when we may go to the head?'

Another believer was convinced that 'it was as good for a man to confess himself alone to God, or else to another layman, as to a priest, upon the saying of St James, where he saith "Show your sins one to another"'. There was also among the Lollards an ethical earnestness which impelled them not only to hear the word of God but also to try to keep it. Some of the early Lollards were vigorous pacifists. Others had a special concern for the poor: 'True pilgrimage,' one Lollard commented, 'is barefoot to go and visit the poor, weak and sick; for they are the true images of God.'

Renewal in Czechoslovakia

The last major medieval renewal movement was the Hussite movement in Czechoslovakia. Unlike the Waldensians and the Wycliffites, the Hussites did not spring into existence independently of other 'heretical' groupings; they were indirectly indebted to both of these predecessors. Yet despite these influences, in a very real sense the Hussites were a distinctive, Czech phenomenon.

In the fourteenth century, spiritual life in Czechoslovakia was becoming more intense. Popular religious writers insisted that the customary annual communion was not enough: all believers, for their souls' health, must participate frequently in the eucharist. There was also a growing appetite for sermons. To meet this demand, the Bethlehem Chapel was erected in Prague in 1394, with seating for 3,000 persons. This chapel quickly became a centre for a style of preaching marked by both anticlericalism and Czech nationalism. Significantly, side by side on its walls were paintings of the pope, resplendent on horseback, and of Jesus, cross-laden on foot.

In 1400, shortly after a conversion experience, John Hus was appointed rector of the Bethlehem Chapel. And during the next twelve years he preached tirelessly, delivering no less than 3,000 sermons. We can tell from his surviving sermon notes that he prepared these with amazing care. Yet he delivered them with fiery freedom in language which the Prague poor could understand. Overflowing congregations warmed to his straightforward instruction, and to his denunciations of an over-endowed, abuse-ridden church.

Wyclif's writings, which were avidly discussed in university circles in Prague at that time, were formative in his thinking; indeed, some of his own writings copy extensively from Wyclif. But Hus was a more cautious, less logical theological thinker than Wyclif. Only in his view of the papacy, which he was convinced had originated at the time of Constantine, did Hus clearly break with medieval orthodoxy. Nevertheless, conservatives felt that his entire ministry was insubordinate and threatening in its tone. In 1412 he was exiled to the South Bohemian countryside, where he led services of worship in barns. And in 1415, at the Council of Constance – despite a safe-conduct, after a rigged trial – he was burned as a heretic.

The burning of Hus rallied the Czech people. In a letter of defiance, 452 Czech nobles declared that Hus had been falsely burnt. Czechs of lesser station were likewise outraged. Religious turbulence began to spread both in Prague and in the countryside. Much of this was associated with the practice of giving to the laypeople at the eucharist both the bread and the chalice rather than solely the bread as in medieval custom. This practice of 'Utraquism' (communion *sub utraque specie*, under both kinds) had been begun by some Hussites as early as 1414, and was a logical expression of the developing Czech concern to breathe new meaning into their communion services. Now Utraquism spread rapidly. Often it was either imposed or repelled by violence.

Utraquism was also linked with other demands and practices, some of them relatively moderate, but others fundamentally challenging the nature of medieval Catholicism. Parties began to form. The moderate Utraquists were content if the word of God could be freely preached, the priests spurned 'pomp, avarice, and improper lordship,' and the church's extensive landholdings were turned over to the people. The radicals wanted to go farther. Many of their concerns – economic sharing, denial of purgatory, refusal of the death penalty – betray their contact with the Waldensians. They had a vigorous belief in the supremacy of the Bible, and a lively expectation that through it God would

speak to them. They met in large numbers, often on South Bohemian hillsides (one of which, renamed Mount Tabor, gave the radicals their name). There they experienced in their times together an intoxicating sense that they were reliving the life of the early Christians. The Taborites listened to powerful preaching, received communion in both kinds (often at the hands of laypeople), and shared their food in 'love feasts'. Many of them believed that the end of the world was at hand.

The birth of the Czech Brethren

Further tensions were inevitable. As the moderate Utraquists tried to consolidate their gains, the radicals became restive. In 1419 they precipitated a revolution in Prague, and in the countryside they turned away from their earlier pacifism.

'The time to wander with a pilgrim's staff is over,' one of them said. 'Now we shall have to march, sword in hand.'

And march the Taborites did, justifying their development of one of the most imposing fighting forces in fifteenth-century Europe by a theology of holy war.

The old city of Prague, where Hus worked for twelve years as rector of Bethlehem Chapel. His preaching was thorough and biblical. He resolutely opposed the claims of the papacy.

Hus was burnt as a heretic after the Council of Constance in 1415, and his ashes were scattered on the Rhine. But the movement for reform continued among the Czech people, and its descendants, like those of the Waldensians and the Lollards, gladly greeted the sixteenth-century Reformation.

For the next fifteen years they were invincible. Indeed, when foreign Catholics attempted to crush the religious independence of the Czech people, it was the Taborites who provided the backbone of the defence. Not until 1434 were they defeated. Then the war-weariness of the people led to a reactionary compromise. The moderates reasserted their dominance, agreeing with the Catholics that the Utraquist lords should be allowed to retain the monastery lands they had expropriated. They concluded that both Utraquism and Catholicism should be tolerated forms of religious expression in Bohemia. Under repression, the exhausted Taborites lost their earlier dynamism and withered away.

In one group, however, the early Taborite longing for a return to primitive Christianity lived on. This was the *Unitas Fratrum* ('Unity of Brothers'), commonly known as the Czech Brethren. The founder of this movement was the Bohemian squire Peter Chelcicky, who died in about 1460. He was grieved when the Taborites turned to 'righteous' violence. Violence, Chelcicky was convinced, is inherently unrighteous. It is a denial of Jesus' teaching, the core of which is the 'Law of Love', and a

repudiation of the practice of Christians before Constantine. State power was necessary, but was ordained by God to be exercised by unbelievers: 'These two divisions, the temporal order of force and Christ's way of love, are far removed from each other,' he wrote. 'For the fullness of authority lies in the accumulation of wealth and vast gatherings of armed men, castles, and walled towns, while the fullness and completion of faith lies in God's wisdom and the strength of the Holy Spirit.' This and other Waldensian themes provided an intellectual basis for a community at Kunwald in north-east Bohemia, in which poverty and community of goods were practised. Late in the century, as the Taborites vanished and the Utraquists fossilized, the Czech Brethren were growing vigorously.

When the Reformation burst upon sixteenth-century Europe, survivors of all these late-medieval renewal movements were forced to make a decision. By and large, the Waldensians, who late in the previous century had surrendered their 300-year-old pacifism to defend their alpine communities, aligned themselves with the Reformation. In 1532, at the synod of Chanforans, they became incorporated into the Reformed international.

The Lollards were more equivocal in their response to the Reformation. Although at first they greeted Protestant preachers and literature warmly, they seem often to have been as uncomfortable with the established Church of England as they had been with medieval Catholicism. The Lollards are thus at the root of subsequent English nonconformity.

By the 1520s, the Utraquists stood for little that was distinctive, and according to preference pledged allegiance either to Roman Catholic or Protestant causes. But the Czech Brethren, unique among all our movements, retained a clearly articulated separate identity. Although they gradually lost their pacifism as the sixteenth century progressed, they continued to have sufficient spiritual stamina to survive bitter persecution by resurgent Catholics in the seventeenth century. They were thus the seed from which the eighteenth-century Moravian Brethren – and much of the modern missionary movement – grew.

Life – bringers

James Atkinson

The Reformers of the sixteenth century were a galaxy of brilliant men of high learning and deep spiritual conviction who flooded the desert wastes of the church with the precious life-giving water of the rivers of God. The greatest of them all – probably the greatest life-bringer to the church since the time of the apostles – was Martin Luther (1483–1546).

Never was there a time when the church needed a Martin Luther as it did then. Never, in all its long history, had the church sunk to such depths of moral obloquy and corruption, or worldliness and unbelief, as it had when Luther was born. To read the diaries kept by the secretary of the Borgia pope, Alexander VI (1493–1503), is to be introduced to a Vatican which was then a world of incest, adultery, prostitution and drunkenness, of gambling and vice, of cynicism and scheming, where bishoprics and cardinalships were sold to the highest bidder, even to boys of eight years old. It was a world as vulgar and vile as the basest of thieves' kitchens, alien to any kind of spirituality, to any kind of theology.

It was Luther who, by preaching and teaching faith based on the Bible and the gospel, gave people a vision of what the Founder Jesus Christ had intended for his church. This clear vision captured the minds of European men and women; it awoke their consciences to how wrong things were. Luther gave people a taste of the old wine of the New Testament, and none who had tasted it ever returned to the new wine of late medieval Catholicism.

History books make a great deal of his work in clearing out wickedness and corruption, yet Luther's concern was not with scandals, but with God. He gave himself to telling a lost world and a straying church what God had done for us in Jesus Christ. He was a man with the gospel. When hearts were convicted and warmed, the scandals fell aside. Luther offered to re-form what mankind had de-formed by giving again to the world the truth in Christ. All his re-forming work was simply to let this same Christ into the church to reform it. In this way Luther is the supreme 'life-giver' of all time. He warms the heart of every man, woman and child who reads him.

Of course, as the previous article has established, there were life-bringers before Luther. God never leaves himself without witness. During the fifteenth and sixteenth centuries a strong anti-papalism and anti-clericalism was simmering in Europe, which the worldliness and increasing financial exactions of the papacy brought to the boil. The German theologian, John of Wesel (1400–81), the Dutch theologian Wessel (c1420–89) – such men, and others like them, have been called, 'Reformers before the Reformation'. The Italian Savanorola (1452–98) was gravely concerned about the moral scandals of the church, less about its theology. But supremely it was England's John Wyclif, whom history has described as 'the morning star of the Reformation', and John Huss of Bohemia who began the work of bringing new life to a despiritualized church.

So Luther stood on prepared ground. Yet still Luther was the Reformation and the Reformation was Luther. He converted all the classical Reformers who followed him, and all Reformers, even the Radicals, took their stance in relation to his pioneer work. Europe was ready for a Luther.

How did it all happen? And what was new about Luther's protest? Why did the whole of Europe, in its political and spiritual dimensions, respond so dramatically to an unknown professor from a new and obscure university?

After graduating with a brilliant law degree at the prestigious university of Erfurt in 1505 at the age of twenty-two, Luther precipitately entered the Augustinian monastery there. He proved to be the perfect monk, and was selected by his superiors to train for a professorship, when after a short period at Erfurt, he was appointed to the new University of Wittenberg in 1511. Here he lectured on the Bible – Genesis, Psalms, Romans, Galatians.

Luther's breakthrough

It was his intense study of the Bible in its original Hebrew and Greek that converted Luther from a scholastic to an evangelical theologian. He was discovering that for all his monastic devotions he was getting no nearer to God. None of the tried ways of discipline, confession and the sacraments

A statue of Martin Luther in the town of Wittenberg, in East Germany. Luther nailed his Ninety-five Theses to the church door in Wittenberg, calling the German people to be faithful to the biblical gospel, and to oppose everything which subverted it.

gave him any certainty about God, and as he studied the Bible, a profound evangelical truth broke through into his mind and soul, and warmed his heart intensely.

Luther had been taught that God was far from mankind, and that by dint of intellect, good works and spiritual exercises men and women must struggle to him. He discovered that it is quite the other way. Mankind is far from God, and in love and forgiveness God came all the way in Christ, and continues so to come. No one has ascended to heaven, but God in Christ came from heaven to earth. When our hearts and minds realize the profundity of this truth, that in relation to God people are nothing and have nothing, we can only stand repentant, and open ourselves up to God to create faith in us. 'By grace you have been saved through faith; and this is not your own doing, it is a gift of God.' So wrote the apostle Paul. As Luther says,

when he saw this, he felt the very gates of Paradise open and he entered.

This, of course, was an old truth, in fact the oldest truth of all, that we are right with God only by God's sovereign grace and love, never by any intrinsic merit or worth of our own. Here is the centre of gospel theology. Yet it was wholly different both from the scholastic teaching of his day and from the church practice of his time. The scholastics taught that a man had to do 'all that in him lay' and to such a man the church ministered her sacraments giving him sufficient grace to prevail.

It was in 1517 that Luther arranged a disputation in the university on the subject of this scholastic theology. Here he gave expression to his new evangelical theology. He spoke of the bondage of sin and deliverance by grace, of Law and of gospel, and of predestination. He put Jesus Christ in the centre of all thinking, but, at the same time, submitted the most devastating

The ancient Lothar Cross has on one side an ornate representation of the Roman Emperor Augustus, and on the other a starkly simple line drawing of the crucified Christ. In his death Jesus cut through all pretensions of power, and set humanity free to live with God. The cross is the greatest symbol of freedom.

criticisms of the theology of his day. As powerful as this disputation was, it was a lesser disputation later that year on the subject of indulgences that fired the imagination of Europe.

At that time the selling of indulgences (remissions from purgatory) was a gross scandal. Apart from the fact that the indulgence in question was a money-raising bazaar to enable Luther's bishop (although too young for any office), to buy the archbishopric from the pope, the malign influence was that the simple folk were taught that they could buy their way out of purgatory, even buy forgiveness for money. It was here that Luther declared the New Testament doctrine of penitence as a total change of heart. From this moment Luther held the world stage.

The next year, 1518, there followed a remarkable chapter at his order at Heidelberg, where, free from controversy, a theologian among believing monks, he opened his heart and declared his new biblical and evangelical theology. The pope sent emissaries 'to quieten down the man', and there followed in 1519 a remarkable debate in Leipzig with the brilliant and redoubtable Catholic controversialist John Eck. This debate showed the irreconcilable split that was emerging between the evangelical Luther and the Catholic church.

When Luther returned home he wrote, among others, three world-shattering books which showed Europe what the coming reformation was concerned to clarify. The first was his *Appeal* in German to the German laity. He struck at the quasi-divine power of Rome, restored the priesthood of all believers, and called for the religious and moral reform of all Christendom. The second was addressed in Latin to the clergy, *The Babylonian Captivity*, wherein Luther severed the tap-root of Romanism, the sacramental system, by which it controlled the laity from the cradle to the grave. The third was a fine, spiritual book on *The Freedom of a Christian Man*. That year he was condemned by a papal bull, which he publicly burned on the town's refuse pit. That deed, on 10 December 1520, when a humble monk, with no more behind him than his faith in God, publicly burned the Pope's bull, proved the firing signal for emancipation throughout Europe: the modern era began at 9 a.m. that day.

He was summoned in April 1521 to the Diet of Worms to recant, but he stood his ground. He was outlawed and excommunicated. On the way home he was captured by friends and imprisoned for his own safety in the Wartburg. There he translated the whole of the New Testament into pure and sublime German within a matter of weeks.

When Luther broke through into the New Testament world of being justified by faith alone, he went through the overwhelming experience of reconciliation with God. He found peace with God, a total

Confined for his own protection in the Wartburg Castle, Saxony, Luther translated the New Testament into German. His faith was above everything a New Testament faith.

explanation of this life and the certainty of joyous life with God for ever. Luther wagered his all on God, and would not be silenced unless proved wrong or shown to be wrong. It was Luther's faith, a faith which throws itself on God, in life and in death, which brought new life to Christendom. Not a speculative or man-centred faith but a faith 'given him by God'. 'Faith is the "Yes" of the heart, a conviction on which one wagers one's life, but it does not arise in us or from us, it is wholly the gift of God . . . On what does faith rest? On Christ . . .' Having faith we have everything: without faith we have nothing.

Christ first and last

It was from such faith kindled by God that Luther was re-created. All his theology derives from this experience. He virtually restored men and women to the place of those who first heard Jesus. Here lay the profound challenge to the Roman Church, to turn to Christ rather than the church, and to stand firm in the priesthood of all believers. He gave the Bible to the people, and opened their eyes not to see it as a mere book, but to read it as a continuous confrontation by God himself. Here was a new (and ultimate) authority, the Word of God, beneath which we all stand, pope and priest alike, princes and peasants too. It was to concede again the ultimate authority of Christ, and to find in him God's love undying for fallen and lost mankind, and to know the joy, the freedom of life in Christ, in his kingdom. Not least, his rediscovery of the church, less as an institution, but as that communion of the faithful, called of God, known only to God. People who knew Luther and lived with him, the students who heard him teach, the Wittenberg folk who heard him preach, the people who received his letters, the folk who read his Bible translation, the people who read his books, all knew that a great prophet and man of God had been given them.

Prophets and messengers from God are welcomed by few. The papists began a long and contrived attack, which eventually culminated in the Council of Trent (1545–63), where a solid basis for the renewal of discipline and spiritual life in the Roman Church was laid, a clear doctrinal basis established and a new religious strength born. The Protestants were anathematized. The Jesuits were ready to roll back the Reformation. Luther was never answered: only condemned. The radicals attacked

Luther for being too conservative, a movement which ultimately expressed itself in the tragic Peasants' War of 1525 which caused grave harm to the Reformation. The humanists were unhappy about the vigorous New Testament theology of Luther, and eventually Erasmus came out against Luther in 1525 with his book *On the Free Will*, in which he attacked Luther's Augustinian theology of grace and the bondage of the will, in favour of humanist doctrine.

Confined to Saxony as an excommunicate and outlaw, Luther worked at Wittenberg to the end of his days, lecturing, writing, preaching and guiding the Reformation. (He wrote a book a fortnight during his last twenty-five years.) He, with others, reorganized the Church of Saxony on evangelical lines, writing catechisms, new liturgical services, composing hymns and educating the ignorant clergy, many of whom could not read. There was nothing he touched, church, university or the common life, but he brought new life into it. He died travelling across Germany in the depth of winter reconciling two squabbling brothers (in February 1545), and was brought home and buried in the church on whose door he had nailed the Ninety-five Theses some twenty-five years earlier.

Ulrich Zwingli

The new movement burst into life all over Europe, sometimes spontaneously and independently of Luther, as in Switzerland. Ulrich Zwingli (1484–1531), a Swiss patriot of Erasmian leanings, was elected minister at Zurich in 1518, where he remained until his death. In this democratic and independent city Zwingli was warmly received by the populace, who liked the young scholar in his search for simplicity of religion. One of the first things he did was to clear out Samson the indulgence seller, when he associated himself with Luther's theology. His first impact was his preaching, which he began at Matthew's Gospel, chapter one, verse one. He virtually moved the congregation of the 'Grossmunster' cathedral from the mass and medieval tradition to the living Word of God expounded by Jesus, the apostles and the prophets. This was the beginning of the Reformation in Switzerland, when Zwingli expounded the New Testament: it was from this unfailing source that Zwingli brought new life into the church. He preached against tithes supporting an excess of clergy, against his countrymen fighting other people's wars as mercenaries. There soon followed attacks on purgatory, the invocation of saints and monasticism.

The papists resisted, but Zwingli called them to two public debates in 1523, where they were ignominiously silenced and routed. The sole basis of truth was the gospel, and once this was granted, the authority of the pope, the sacrifices of the mass, the invocation of saints, times and seasons of fasting, and clerical celibacy were rejected.

It was at this stage Zwingli developed his characteristic eucharistic teaching (sometimes called Zwinglianism). He rejected both the Roman teaching and Luther's ideas, adopting a more radical position. This theology produced a tragic break with Luther in 1529.

In his *Commentary on True and False Religion* (1525) Zwingli revealed his full theology. He first established the source of all true religion as the Word of God. Any other religion is false and mere superstition. Central to all his evangelical theology is Christ. He treats of forgiveness and penitence, of Law and sin, and of the true gospel. He handles church and sacraments: the church is not the hierarchy but the community of called and believing people; the sacraments are signs and symbols of God's loving relation to humanity. Confession, marriage, vows, invocation of saints, images, prayer, purgatory are all critically examined in the light of his evangelical theology.

The movement began to spread through Switzerland. In a public debate at Berne (1528), Zwingli successfully held his ground and the city joined the Reformation. Basel, St Gall and others followed. In Constance the bishop and his clergy ignominiously withdrew and left it all to the Reformers.

Nevertheless, the movement met fierce resistance, particularly in the Forest Cantons. Unable to win by debate, the Catholics turned to the sword. They captured and burned a Zurich pastor. Zwingli saw war on the horizon. The Lutherans would not recognize him. The Emperor refused to listen to him. He found little material support anywhere. The Catholics attacked. Unprepared for war, and heavily outnumbered, Zwingli perished on the field of battle at Kappel in

Ulrich Zwingli was people's priest at Grossmünster, the cathedral of Zurich, Switzerland. His systematic preaching from the New Testament gradually won the people over to a message which emphasized the centrality of personal faith.

1531, as chaplain to the Protestants: he fell with their standard in his hand. His helmet, with the horrible gash caused by that fatal blow, may still be seen in the museum at Zurich, together with his New Testament which he was carrying in his belt as he fell. Yet the cause did not fail. It was taken up in Geneva by the learned and austere Calvin, the reluctant Reformer, quite literally seized by God and established in Geneva.

John Calvin

It is a strange and dramatic story how John Calvin (1509–64) was thrust into the leadership of the Reformation. Compelled to leave the University of Paris in 1533 for his Lutheran views, an exile from his native land, he settled in Basel, a city peopled by learned humanists and theologians of the reformed persuasion, such as Erasmus, Myconius and Bullinger. Here he published his *Institutes*, and here he intended to pursue a quiet life of scholarship and writing.

Passing through Geneva to settle his father's estate, the fiery Reformation preacher, Guillaume Farel, called on Calvin. He carried the startling news that Calvin was sent by God to teach and preach, and that if he disobeyed the divine commission, he would have to face God on the day of judgement and answer him. Calvin was greatly disturbed, and after a night of anguish, realized that Farel had simply told him the truth. Calvin took over the Reformation in Geneva. He converted the rabble of the Reformation into a disciplined army. Whereas Luther's liberating genius was restricted to Saxony,

An old map of Geneva, where John Calvin taught and worked for many years. He wanted to establish there a holy city, with the whole municipal life and law based on the teaching of the Bible.

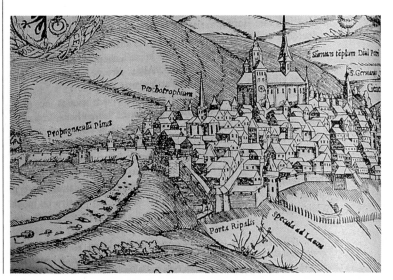

from Geneva Calvin was to influence Europe. The Reformation needed a Calvin. His was a genius as great as Luther's, but of a totally different kind. Luther, a warm-hearted extrovert, full of humour and homely wit, was free and open to everyone, a great liberator and communicator; Calvin was dark, close, silent, with a genius for organization and systematization. Luther did what Calvin could never have done: Calvin did what Luther could never have done.

In Geneva he faced his master problem. How could the church be made not simply an institution for worshipping God, but an agency for making people fit to worship him? He established a regime based on the rule of God. He realized that the reformed faith could live in a democratic and free city only by an enlightened pulpit speaking to enlightened citizens, and that an educated ministry needed an educated laity. He created both.

Nevertheless, in all essentials he stood at one with the other Reformers: though he had different emphases, he was always biblical and evangelical. One marked difference between him and Luther, a difference which comes out in their theology, is that whereas Luther approached God and found him gracious, Calvin started with the sovereignty of God. Calvin felt mastered by God, that his will was God's, to do with him as he pleased or needed. He was God-possessed, God-mastered, even God-intoxicated: Calvin's theology arises from this passionate God-centredness.

A consequence of this was his emphasis on humanity's hopeless corruption, and God's work in election and predestination; on God's mercy and not mankind's merit or effort. This was a direct challenge to Rome's claims to authority and finality. The basis of everything was not Rome, but the objective fact of God's decree in Christ; certainty and assurance lay in God alone and not in the church at all.

He held the same high doctrine of the Bible as all the Reformers did. Scripture to him was inerrant, in that no more was included than was required, and no less given than was needed. It was also sufficient, in that all that was required was in the Bible. The corollary was true: what was in the Bible needed to be known. The Scriptures revealed all that a person can know about God, and all that he must know. Calvin did not mean this as some kind of passive assent. There must be a change of mind and heart before approaching the Bible; we must allow God to give us the right understanding through the internal testimony of the Holy Spirit. In regarding Scripture as this self-authenticating unity, Calvin was providing an authority beyond reason, conscience or the secular power, all of which may err.

When Calvin came to formulate an evangelical doctrine of the church there were three views abroad. The Roman view was hierarchical: to be a Christian was to be in communion with Rome, the guardian of truth and morals. Luther saw the true church as the elect of God: a community known only to God, though manifest in the world nevertheless, and which had for its head Christ alone. The Anabaptists conceived of the church as a society of the redeemed, gathered out of the world, and keeping itself pure by excommunicating the disobedient. An important aspect was how these three views saw themselves in relation to social authority. The Roman position was rather ill-defined; its authority was closely allied with the civil authority, but in fact superior to it. Luther rested authority not in the church but in the prince: there were two kingdoms, never to be confused. The Anabaptists repudiated any and every relation with the state or with secular society.

Calvin took over elements of all three. With Luther he emphasized the true church as hidden, made up, as Augustine had taught, of the chosen people of God. With the Catholics he held that the visible church is of vital importance; but he argued further that it must show forth the principles of Reformation theology, and that its relation to the state was definite and independent. With the Anabaptists he insisted on a rigorous public discipline of all members of the church, though rejecting the idea of a 'gathered' community: Calvin would not separate the elect from the visible church as a distinct community. Calvin is sometimes described as seeking to establish a 'theocracy': a community based on the rule of God. It is nearer the truth to say that he sought independence of the state in the government of her own affairs, yet made the highest demands on the temporal authority. His views on church and state were complementary.

With Calvin the Reformation movement was finalized and given a system. Simple and austere, sometimes intolerant, even vindictive, he lacked all the humanity and warmth of Luther. Nevertheless, his

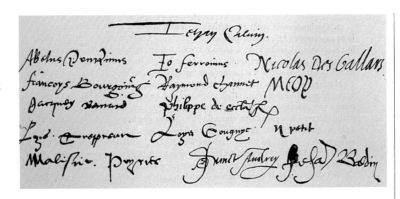

influence was and is enormous. His theological insight, his exegetical talents, his lucid and pithy style, his extraordinary capacity to systematize and expound, have made him the most influential of all the Reformers. He was a great life-bringer to the church, and remains so to this day.

The English Church

As far as England was concerned the Reformation at first was a Lutheran movement which brought life to the suppressed Wycliffites. Barnes, Tyndale, Cranmer, Ridley and Latimer, and all the early Reformers, learned their theology from Luther. A strong Luther society existed in Cambridge. In Oxford, as early as 1520, Luther's books were on sale. Henry VIII's theologians held conversations in Wittenberg, mainly (but not only) in 1535–36. Certain advances were made during his reign: articles of an evangelical nature were written in 1536 and 1538; the Bible set up in churches in 1538; evangelical injunctions promulgated by Thomas Cromwell in 1538; the

The signatures of the pastors of Geneva, attached to a declaration passed by the 'congregation of brothers' in 1547. Calvin's signature is at the top.

Old Sodbury Manor House, in Gloucestershire, England, where William Tyndale did some of the work on his English Bible. It is remarkable how often translating the Bible into the common tongue has led to a great increase in a people's search for freedom.

In the reign of Queen Mary many Protestants were burned as heretics. Thomas Cranmer was pressed to recant, and at first did so. But when he withdrew his recantation his enemies were enraged. They pulled him down from the dais, took him out and had him burnt.

Institution of a Christian Man drawn up in 1537. Many other changes came about such as the destruction of shrines and images and a more evangelical organization of church life.

It was not until the reign of Edward VI (1547–53) that the great change took place. Cranmer's *Homilies* appeared, Erasmus' *Paraphrases* were set up in the churches, and further *Injunctions* issued to the clergy, and Cranmer wrote the *Book of Common Prayer*. Many other changes were made such as the dissolution of chantries, the setting up of schools and hospitals, the destruction of images and the abolition of catholic devotional practices. Cranmer was clearly looking to reform Catholicism.

When the young king died, Mary (1553–58) repealed all reform laws and sought to restore Roman Catholicism. She actually burned some 300 Protestants, including Cranmer and all the leading theologians who did not escape her. Her desperate and unhappy reign lasted only for five years. She was succeeded by Elizabeth (1558–1603) who, with her theologians, gave Britain the Protestant religious settlement. She had a desperate struggle both against treasonable Catholic plots and intrigue many centring round the Catholic Mary Queen of Scots, as well as against Puritanism (a rigorous form of Calvinism), but she prevailed. Here two theologians played a leading part: John Jewel and Richard Hooker.

John Jewel opposed both the Roman Catholics and the Puritans, taking his stand on the early Church Fathers of the first six centuries. In 1562 he published his famous *Apology of the Church of England*, where he showed the necessity of reform and the justification of provincial reformation when Rome will not reform. Among a number of poor boys whom Jewel maintained was one Richard Hooker who, when he grew up to manhood, completed his patron's work in his masterly *Ecclesiastical Polity* 1594–97. He was the most accomplished advocate Anglicanism has ever had. He opposed the Puritans for their biblical literalism. He argued that the church was a living not a static institution, and that its government and administration at any time must change according to historical necessity. He argued that the Anglican Church, now reformed, had continuity with the medieval church, even the early church. He accepted the non-episcopal orders of Continental Protestantism: the succession may have been regretfully broken, but he saw apostolic succession as a succession of apostolic doctrine not as a matter of lineage.

This was and has remained the definitive Anglican position. In respect of comprehension it finally broke down in the Act of Uniformity of 1662, when Anglicanism was imposed on the country by law, and when the Presbyterians and Independents, with all their fine theology and religious conviction, were finally and tragically lost to the national church. Nevertheless, the Church of England stands by its Reformation Formularies, its Articles and its Prayer Book, in which our Anglican divines reformed the historic catholic church of this realm. This idea of *reformed* Catholicism, wholly independent of the papacy, was based on Scripture, tradition and reason, allowing all matters of government and administration to national custom and natural law.

For four and a half centuries Rome has fulminated against the Protestants and anathematized all its theologians. It is only since the Second Vatican Council (1962–65) that Roman Catholic scholars (and to some extent church leaders), are beginning to see that the Reformers were the great life-bringers to the church. They are not to be condemned and excommunicated. They should be seen as men sent by God to reform a church desperately in need of reformation. They brought and still bring life to the church, fresh life from God.

God's left wing

Alan Kreider

On a January evening in 1525, in the Zurich rooms of Felix Manz, one of the city's most promising Hebrew scholars, a remarkable event took place. An upper-class theology student named Conrad Grebel turned to a rough-hewn priest from the Tyrol, George Cajacob, and baptized him. Then, along with the other men gathered in the room (on this occasion there seem to have been no women present), Grebel received baptism from Cajacob. 'In the high fear of God' and with a deep bond of 'togetherness', the brothers then solemnly committed themselves to the Lord and to each other, and they emerged 'to teach and keep the faith'. With this event, the first believer's baptism since the church's early centuries, the Anabaptist movement began, and with it the nonconformist tradition within Protestantism.

What had compelled these men to take this extraordinary action? It was not simply their growing theological antipathy to infant baptism. More fundamentally, they were motivated by a desire for a more far-reaching reformation of the church in Zurich than the city council would allow. In the early stages of the Zurich reformation, it had not appeared that this would be an insuperable problem. Ulrich Zwingli, the city's reformer from 1519 onwards, had successfully coped with conservative opposition by both disputation and negotiation, and the Anabaptists-to-be were among his most committed supporters. They had been drawn to his message of faith and the centrality of the word and work of Christ. They had been stirred when he announced that 'to be a Christian is not to talk about Christ, but to walk as He walked.' They had been intrigued by his iconoclastic speculations, such as that 'it would be much better that children should have their . . . baptism when they reach an appropriate age'. With him they had studied the Bible in small house-fellowship-like 'schools'; and when he on Ash Wednesday 1522 had eaten 'forbidden fruit' (pork sausages) they had joined with him.

But by 1523 tensions were evident which two years later would lead to a parting of the ways. The City Councillors, sensing that changes had been taking place too fast for comfort, began to balk at new measures of reformation, such as the granting of the cup to the laity in the mass. Zwingli was inclined to hide his exasperation and to wait for the authorities to change their minds, but his radical disciples were less patient. At stake was an issue which they were gradually coming to see was fundamental. Whose decision should govern the life and policy of the church? The City Councillors or the Spirit of God speaking through the Bible? Zwingli's reluctant preference was for the former, so that religious change might take place responsibly and uniformly. For, according to customary medieval assumptions which Zwingli accepted, the religious unity of a territory was the guarantee of its civic welfare.

Those who felt that religious decisions should be taken by groups of earnest believers interpreting the Bible on their own, on the other hand, were entering uncharted territory. A new vision of the church was emerging among the Anabaptists-to-be, tentatively, amid debate and deep inner searching. It would be a church, not of the multitudes, but of the 'few . . . believing and walking aright' on a path of social nonconformity; a church uncoupled from the state's coercion, and avoiding all participation in violence; a church of those who had chosen to be disciples and who would follow their Master into 'anguish and affliction'. In such a church there would be no place for what appeared to them to be the coerciveness of infant baptism.

Persecution and growth

Conrad Grebel had sensed that 'Christ must still suffer more in his members'. Shortly the movement of which he was a part discovered the reality of his premonition. A few hours before the first baptisms in January 1525, the Zurich City Council had forbidden the radicals to meet. From the very start therefore, their meetings were acts of civil disobedience.

As the Anabaptists began with missionary fervour to reach out into the surrounding areas – preaching, baptizing and forming congregations – they continued to encounter severe opposition from the civil authorities. When it was seen that imprisonment and banishment were ineffective in stemming the spread of

Anabaptism, governments resorted to execution. In May 1525 the first Anabaptist was executed – by burning – by Catholic authorities in Schwyz. The first Anabaptist to be executed by Protestants was the Hebraist Felix Manz, in whose rooms that first baptism had happened. In early 1527 he was drowned in Zurich's Limmat River, protesting that those who executed him were 'destroying the very essence of Christianity'. Despite the severity of the repression and the fact that by 1529 most of the early Anabaptist leaders had died, in the early 1530s Zwingli's successor Bullinger was writing that 'people are running after them as if they were the living saints'.

By this time the movement was not confined to Switzerland. This was not solely because the Swiss Brethren had fanned out with their message into South Germany and the Tyrol and were soon to reach Moravia. At the same time, in response to similar circumstances, other groups of Anabaptists were springing into existence. Some of these, such as the South German congregations associated with the ex-Benedictine prior Michael Sattler and the theologian Balthasar Hubmaier, quickly established relationships of varying degrees of closeness with the Swiss Brethren. But others, in central Germany and the Netherlands, were too far afield to have had any connection whatsoever with the Swiss, and had apparently sprung up spontaneously.

This is not surprising, for the conditions which produced Anabaptism were common in many parts of Europe. Religious expectancy and restlessness were superimposed on a sense of economic grievance; in South Germany Anabaptism spread in the wake of the suppression of the Peasants' Revolt. In many places Anabaptism reflected disenchantment with the fruits of the official Reformation. According to one believer from Bern, among the Reformers, despite their doctrinal changes, 'true repentance and Christian love were not in evidence'.

Anabaptism also spread as a result of the tireless activity of preachers. The major Reformers still accepted Jesus' 'Great Commission' to preach the gospel to the whole world. But since they continued to accept without question the medieval idea that church and society were one and the same, they were reluctant to apply the Commission to their own situations. The Anabaptists, on the other hand, had no such reservations. Their deep missionary consciousness is evident in their court hearings; there is no text that they quoted more often than the Great Commission. Like the apostles, they felt themselves called to unauthorized preaching. Some of this was tumultuous, and much of it, especially in the early years, was quite uncoordinated. Indeed, the earliest Anabaptist missionaries were often 'sent' primarily by the civil authorities who had banished them. But soon the preachers began to co-ordinate their activities. In Augsburg in 1527, a 'martyr synod' (most of the preachers present were soon executed) met to divide South Germany among the missioners. And by the early 1530s the Hutterite communities in Moravia were carefully planning the sending of missionary teams into various parts of Europe.

A violent aberration

The expected second coming of Jesus was yet another spur to the spread of Anabaptism. In the early sixteenth century many people sensed that they were living in the last days. Martin Luther, for example, hurriedly translated the book of Daniel 'so that everyone might read and comprehend it before the end of the world'. Anabaptists often shared this vivid expectancy, and – especially since they were experiencing severe persecution – it added an immediacy to their preaching which was attractive to many. Some Anabaptists made calculations about the end of the world, and a few of these were convinced that when Jesus returned his otherwise non-violent disciples would be

The Anabaptists were severely persecuted by the mainline Reformers, so that they often had to meet in secret. This still happens to some Christian groups whose teaching does not fit the ideas of dominant state authorities. This small group is meeting in secret in a wood outside their town.

justified in taking up arms against the unrighteous.

In the Westphalian episcopal city of Münster, one such group of Anabaptists forcibly seized power in 1534. As the non-resident bishop massed troops and besieged the city, the inhabitants – believing that the millennium had come – defended themselves with arms. They began to behave in a way that was extraordinary for the Anabaptist movement at large. The believers received direct revelations; they linked the church with the state; they viewed the Old Testament as normative for ethics, justifying polygamy. When Münster fell in 1535 amid starvation and slaughter, speculation about the last days fell into disrepute among those parts of the Anabaptist movement that had earlier engaged in it.

To many Protestant and Catholic contemporaries, the debacle of Münster came – to the exclusion of everything else – to express the essence of Anabaptism. They therefore felt justified in intensifying the persecution of Anabaptists wherever they could ferret them out. Anabaptism had, of course, been illegal all along. Local proscriptions had been generalized by the 1529 Diet of Speyer, at which the Evangelicals (now for the first time called 'Protestants') and Catholics agreed on one thing – that those who baptized believers or were 're-baptized' should be subject to the death penalty. Anabaptist, or 're-baptizer', is thus a term coined by their enemies, to sanction persecution under an ancient imperial law condemning the Donatists; the Anabaptists preferred to be called 'brothers and sisters'.

Throughout the sixteenth century persecution thus continued to be severe. Informers were planted in Anabaptist meetings; a special imperial police force ('Baptist-hunters') was recruited to pursue the heretics; and inquisitors were expressly trained to cow them back to orthodoxy. Inquisitors were assisted by torture – 'severe examination', as it was euphemistically called. There were thousands of executions, as many as 2,500 in the Netherlands alone. Martyrdom thus became a theme of the Anabaptist movement, celebrated in hymns and recounted at length in the massive martyrology which for centuries has given the descendants of the Anabaptists their self-identity, *Martyrs' Mirror*.

Münster was a disaster for the Anabaptist movement, but good came out

Menno Simons, from Frisia in the Netherlands, was the Anabaptist leader whose name is most widely remembered today. Mennonite Christians follow his teaching.

of it. For it led to the conversion of a Frisian priest, Menno Simons, who identified himself with the harassed Anabaptists and who determined to lead them back on to the path of non-violent discipleship which had predominated in the movement. This was a costly decision. From 1536 until his death in 1561, Menno was on the run, shepherding scattered flocks from Holland into Germany, preaching by night, and writing tracts which he printed on the rudimentary press which he lugged on his travels. With a touch of bitterness he contrasted his lot with that of the preachers of the now-established Protestant churches:

'I with my poor, weak wife and children have for years endured excessive anxiety, oppression, affliction, and persecution . . . Yes, when the preachers repose on easy beds and soft pillows, we generally have to hide ourselves in out-of-the-way corners . . . We have to be on our guard when a dog barks for fear the arresting officer has arrived . . . In short, while they are gloriously rewarded for their services with large incomes and good times, our recompense and portion be but fire, sword and death.'

Thanks in significant measure to Menno's courageous pastoring and resolute pacifist commitment, an Anabaptist movement survived in Northern Europe. For good reason it, like many of the descendants of the brethren in Switzerland and South Germany, came to be known as 'Mennonite'.

Community of goods

In Moravia, however, local manifestation of the Anabaptist movement came to be known as 'Hutterite', after an early leader,

Jakob Hutter (burned in 1536). The Hutterites were distinguished from the Swiss Brethren and from the North-European Mennonites by their insistence on community of goods. Since Christians held spiritual things in common, one Hutterite reasoned, so they ought also to have communion in material things 'that as Paul says . . . there may be equality'. Only by relinquishing private possessions and entering a community (*Bruderhof*) could they truly express their love for God and their fellow Christians.

Although Hutterite Anabaptists did indeed give up private property, in the course of the sixteenth century their communities in Moravia and Hungary became wealthy and large – at one point they apparently had up to 30,000 members. Each Bruderhof was superbly organized. As one brother testified, 'it is like a beehive where all the busy bees work together to a common end, the one doing this, the other that, not for their own need but for the good of all'. the brothers developed handcrafts and light industry to a high level; their education was so excellent that local nobles sent their children to the communities for schooling; and the skill of Hutterite physicians made them in demand at the imperial court.

The Hutterites were resolute nonconformists (throughout the sixteenth century, for example, the Bruderhofs refused to pay war taxes). This and their manifest prosperity soon excited the envy and hostility of their neighbours. In 1595 the first of many blows fell, bringing their Golden Period to an end amid severe persecution. After waves of confiscation and repression, a few Hutterites, their 'beehives' broken up, survived by migrating to the Ukraine.

The Anabaptist movement was thus diverse. Indeed, a movement that was decentralized and persecuted, that extended from Holland to Hungary, and that contained a high proportion of 'movement-type' personalities, was bound to produce a variety of emphases. But despite these diversities, many of which worked their way out of the movement within its first decade, the number of uniformities that appear is striking. There was a bedrock of vision that set the Radicals off from the other Reformers and that made Anabaptism a distinctive Christian tradition of enduring significance.

On many points, to be sure, the Anabaptists were in agreement with the Reformers. The main contours of their theology were orthodox, and they were deeply influenced by Luther's writings. Some of them were personal friends of Zwingli and Bucer. Yet their emphases were distinctive, so perversely so (it seemed to Reformers and Catholics alike) that the Anabaptists must be banished or executed.

To some extent, the distinctiveness of the Anabaptists' vision resulted from their way of 'doing theology'. When people are being persecuted and oppressed, they tend to have a different perspective on God, the world, and the Bible from those who have positions of power in state-supported universities or churches. The Anabaptists' circumstances of writing also determined the literary forms that their theological writing could take. Lacking safety, leisure and libraries, they naturally did not write systematic theologies or learned commentaries; they (like the early Christians, writing in a similar setting) wrote letters, narratives and controversial pieces.

Most Anabaptists, of course, could not have written academic theology if they had tried. Only one of the early Anabaptists, Balthasar Hubmaier, had a doctorate in theology, and he was burned in 1528. Thanks to persecution, by the 1530s Anabaptist theology was being written almost entirely by laymen. Some of it, written by the civil engineer Pilgram Marpeck, was perceptive and original. But the striking thing about Anabaptist theology is not the brilliance of the individual writers; it is rather, as letters and court records testify, the deep knowledge many Anabaptists had of the Bible. In court hearings Anabaptist women (as in most renewal movements, women were especially active among the early Anabaptists) could confound their inquisitors with a superb command of the texts. As one exasperated inquisitor blurted out, 'Why do you trouble yourself with Scripture? Attend to your sewing!' Another priest exclaimed in dumbfounded admiration, 'You Anabaptists are certainly fine fellows to understand the holy Scriptures; for before you are rebaptized, you can't tell A from B, but as soon as you are baptized, you can read and write!'

Brothers and sisters

What then were the emphases which gave these lay theologians their distinctiveness, and which Reformers and Romanists alike found it impossible to tolerate? I have already mentioned the first – the Anabaptists' insistence that since faith is God's gift, religious compulsion is an offence against him. The early Luther (1522) had stated that he would 'constrain no man by force, for faith must come freely without compulsion'. Although Luther soon changed his mind, the Anabaptists persisted with this insight. 'Christ's people,' one of them said, 'are a free, unforced, and uncompelled people, who receive Christ with desire and a willing heart.'

This logic led them, in advance of their contemporaries, to espouse religious toleration. 'A Turk or a heretic,' Hubmaier pleaded, 'cannot be persuaded by us either with the sword or with fire, but only with patience and prayer.' This logic also led them to reject infant baptism, which appeared to them to be an act of adult compulsion committed on an unconsenting infant. And the consequence of compulsion, they came to recognize, was a society which, though superficially Christian, was largely made up of slightly Christianized pagans. That the church was established, and a region's religion was

determined by its prince, simply compounded the problem.

The voluntarist Anabaptists were thus attacking the form of the 'Christian' social order which had dominated Europe ever since Constantine had legalized Christianity and Theodosius I had made it compulsory. Unlike the Reformers, the Anabaptists not only wanted to restore biblical norms in doctrine; they wanted as well to restore the sociology, the ethics and the missionary dynamic of the early Christians – even if it meant powerlessness and suffering.

A second Anabaptist emphasis followed logically from the first: the church is a family of believers. Basic to the composition of the Believers' Church is conversion. One enters it by rebirth (about which the Anabaptists talked and wrote at length) rather than by birth. And since it was a product of 'regeneration which is performed by the Spirit of God', this new, non-genetic family was the most important social unit to which anyone could belong. In the Middle Ages, priests had expressed their solidarity by calling one another 'brothers'; so likewise spoke the pastors in the state churches of the Reformation. But

One group of Mennonites in the United States is the Old Order Amish. They have refused to compromise with a number of aspects of modern life. They still use the older, pre-mechanized methods of farming.

all members of Anabaptist congregations called each other 'sisters and brothers'. They were conscious that they were all members of a priesthood of believers, not only in status but in function. They did, to be sure, have leaders, whom they called 'shepherds' or 'servants of the Word'. But these leaders must be servants like themselves, whose calling it was to 'take care of the body of Christ, that it may be built up and developed'.

This corporate, family consciousness shaped every area of Anabaptist life. For example, it gave a special character to their worship. In their meetings, every member was important. Unlike the other Reformers, the Anabaptists were convinced that God had never withdrawn the gifts of the Holy Spirit from the church. As a Swiss brother wrote in the 1530s, 'when some one comes to church and constantly hears only one person speaking, and all the listeners are silent, neither speaking nor prophesying, who can regard the same to be a spiritual congregation, or confess according to 1 Corinthians 14 that God is dwelling and operating in them?' So in an Anabaptist meeting, speaker would follow speaker, corroborating an earlier message or adding new insights as the Spirit gave lead. Other members would participate in the prayers, in transacting congregational business, and in sharing with the needy from the common fund. These meetings, which because of persecution were often held at night in forests or homes, could get lengthy. Near Strasbourg a congregation appointed a member to circulate throughout the meeting carrying a lantern, jostling anyone who had dozed off and whispering, 'Wake up, brother!'

For the Anabaptists, this self-giving within the body always had economic consequences. Among the Hutterites it led, as we have seen, to total community of goods. Like the other Anabaptists, the Hutterites were acutely conscious of the division that could be caused in congregations by a disparity of wealth. Their solution was equality. 'In brief,' Ulrich Stadler observed, '*one, common* builds the Lord's house and is pure; but *mine, thine, his, own* divides the Lord's house and is impure.' The other Anabaptist traditions, on the other hand, sought to build up the common life by a vigorous programme of mutual aid. Many congregations had common purses, to which members could voluntarily contribute according to their ability and from which other members could draw in time of need. There was also apparently much informal sharing. Whatever the method, the Anabaptists were convinced that economic sharing was an evidence that a loving God was at work among his people.

A final indication of the importance that the Anabaptists accorded to the integrity of the corporate life is indicated by their practice of church discipline. The heart of this lay in what they called 'the rule of Christ', which committed each member to deal with sin or difficult relationships on a one-to-one basis. If neither that nor a larger deputation led to reconciliation, the matter would be brought, not to the minister, but to the congregation. If the body found that one party had sinned, it would exercise the ban ('the power of fraternal punishment'). The Anabaptists insisted that they did this 'with a sorrowing heart', for redemptive purposes. 'We do not want to amputate,' Menno claimed, 'but rather to heal; not to discard, but to win back.'

Following after

The Anabaptists' third distinctive emphasis was discipleship, which they called *Nachfolge* ('following after'). A Christian, according to Menno, was a person who 'willingly walks in the footsteps of Christ'. Through repentance he has received God's pardon, which will inevitably be 'in evidence by newness of life in Christ'. The disciple must thus be experiencing both internal and external transformation; and his inward renewal must be leading to a change of lifestyle – to 'amendment of life' according to the model and teaching of Jesus. Indeed, as Hans Denck expressed it in the most characteristic sentence ever penned by an Anabaptist, 'No one can truly know Christ unless he follows him in life.'

Following Jesus was in part a matter of imitating him. The Anabaptists, for obvious reasons, placed a strong emphasis on the Gospel narratives. They were convinced that 'the plain and simple will of God is that we hold before our eyes his dear Son, Jesus Christ, and follow his life and teaching' (Hubmaier). Sometimes they called this imitation 'conformity to Christ', which they almost always linked to suffering. From prison one Anabaptist conveyed to his fellow believers what he had discerned the Lord to be saying to the church: 'If I the Lord and Master am poor, it is evident that my servants are poor, and that my disciples do not seek or desire riches . . . He that would follow me, must follow me in the poverty in which I walk before him.'

To imitation the Anabaptists added obedience. They found it unthinkable that Jesus' commandments, difficult though they seemed to put into practice, should apply only to attitudes and not to actions. 'Why should God make known his will,' Michael Sattler reasoned, 'if he would not wish that a person do it . . . Christ makes known to us the true obedience by which alone the Father is satisfied.' Indeed, obedience is necessary to make sense of belief in the body of Christ. For it is unthinkable that there should be ethical dis-coordination in the body. 'As Christ our head is minded, so also must be minded the members of the body of Christ through him, so that there be no division in the body.'

Obedience to Jesus as the Anabaptists conceived it, however, was costly. Since he had not preached 'easy and sweet things', he was leading them into behaviour that was unconventional and that contemporaries could construe as being subversive. Conflict with the authorities followed. On the issue of the swearing of oaths, for example, the approach of most Anabaptists was clear. As Menno put it, 'If you fear the Lord and are asked to swear, continue in the Lord's Word which has forbidden you so plainly to swear, and let your yea and nay be your oath as was commanded, whether life or death be your lot.' Jesus had given this teaching, the Anabaptists were convinced, because he wanted his disciples without constraint to tell the truth all of the time; for them there must be no gradation between levels of honesty. The Anabaptists' Catholic and Protestant critics feared, however, that by refusing the oath the Anabaptists were not only rejecting the legal system; they were also undercutting the social order by avoiding the compulsory oaths of loyalty which most territorial princes annually required of their subjects. If the Anabaptists' ideas of obedience were to spread, what prince or legal system would be secure?

Subversives?

It was probably in the area of warfare that Anabaptist ideas of obedience to Jesus seemed most threatening. In the mid-sixteenth century, Protestants and Catholics alike were terrified by the seemingly inexorable military advance of the Turks, who were besieging Vienna and seemed determined to snuff out Christian civilization in Europe. Although a few

Some of the radical groups used ingenious forms of meeting to avoid detection and arrest. An Amsterdam ferryman, Pieter Pieters, made his boat available for groups of people to meet and teach one another.

early Anabaptists held Just War or holy war positions, the majority – even in the face of the Turk – were pacifists. As the martyr Felix Manz put it, 'The true love of Christ shall scatter the enemy; so that he who would be an heir with Christ is taught that he must be merciful, as the Father in heaven is merciful.' The Anabaptists' forthrightness in this area could occasionally chill their hearers. Shortly before his burning in 1527, the pacifist Michael Sattler responded to the inevitable question, 'What about the Turks?' with the riposte: 'If waging war were proper, I would rather take the field against the so-called Christians who persecute, take captive, and kill true Christians, than against the Turks.'

Language of this sort was inflammatory; some Anabaptists would not have approved of it. Nevertheless, virtually all Anabaptists had an attitude to political power which deviated from the sixteenth-century norm. They often quoted the apostle Paul to emphasize obedience to the civil authorities, but they always added a significant – and they felt biblical – proviso, 'when not contrary to the Word of God'. They also tended to be less elaborately deferential to their rulers than were most of their contemporaries. In one hearing, for example, although the City Recorder verbally genuflected to the judges as 'provident, honourable and wise lords', the Anabaptist in the dock repeatedly addressed them simply as 'ye servants of God'.

Many Anabaptists, both because of their conscience against taking life and because of the persecution which they were experiencing, concluded that it was not possible for a faithful Christian to participate in government. There cannot be, these Anabaptists felt, any overlapping between the kingdom of God and the kingdom of this world. 'The world uses the sword; Christians use only spiritual weapons.' Other Anabaptists were more cautious, contending that 'it is difficult for a Christian to be a temporal ruler'. It was difficult because of Jesus' commandments, to which even rulers who would be Christian were subject. So it was possible for Christians to participate in government, one Anabaptist commented, if they 'take upon themselves the cross, and give up force and splendour'.

For most sixteenth-century rulers and churchmen, persecution was the natural expression of their fears of subversion. The Anabaptists did not enjoy this. 'It is not convenient,' one of them stated plaintively, 'to be burnt.' Indeed, many of them devised ingenious means of avoiding arrest; there are some marvellous Anabaptist escape stories! But there are also stories – hundreds of stories, told in loving detail – of suffering, consciously chosen and courageously faced. One of the most famous of these is that of the Dutchman Dirk Willems, who in 1569 by scrambling across thin ice had successfully escaped from the thiefcatcher who was pursuing him. When he got to the other side, however, he saw that his pursuer had broken through the ice and was desperately pleading for help. Dirk turned around and pulled him to safety, whereupon the thiefcatcher's superior, standing safely on the other bank, shouted across to the dripping thiefcatcher and, 'very sternly compelling him to consider his oath', forced him to arrest the man who had just saved his life. This time Dirk did not run. Shortly thereafter, after torture, by means of a 'lingering fire', Dirk was executed.

The suffering of Dirk and his many brothers and sisters was intense, but within the framework of Anabaptist theology it made sense. It had always been the case, the Anabaptists were convinced, 'that those who would live godly in Christ Jesus have had to suffer persecution'. Repeatedly they reminded themselves that Jesus had assured his disciples, 'The servant is not greater than his Master. They have persecuted me; so will they persecute you.' The Anabaptists were certain that this promise, which the early Christians had found to be precious, had not ceased to be valid. Indeed, suffering seemed to them a sign that the church was being faithful to the One who had called them to take up their crosses and to follow him. From their perspective, there could be no true church that was not a 'church under the Cross'.

Alternative forms of society

Constantly under pressure as they were, the Anabaptists were tempted to become cankered and contrary. There was indeed some bitterness and negativism among them. But among them too – even amid persecution – there was a confidence, expectation and joy rooted in their experience of God at work among them. They had the strange confidence that through their missionary activities God could renew European society. As Menno put it, 'We preach, as much as is possible, both by night and by day, in houses and in fields, before lords and princes, through mouth and pen, with possessions and blood, with life and death. For we feel his living fruit and moving power in our hearts, as may be seen in many places by the loving patience and willing sacrifices of our faithful brethren. We could wish that we might save all mankind from the chains of their sins . . .'

But converted men and women could never exist on their own. Central to the Anabaptist social strategy was therefore the church. They knew that it was useless to renew society by seizing the reins of power, legislating laws that were as righteous as possible, and coercing those who were recalcitrant. This strategy, they felt, had been tried many times throughout the history of Constantinian Christendom, and had failed because it was superficial. It did not lead to true faithfulness to Christ's teaching. For true righteousness could not be compelled; it could come about only as men and women discovered the meaning of

One great emphasis of the Radical Reformers was their refusal to bear arms. (The incident at Münster was an isolated deviation.) They believed this was the stance of the early Christians.

repentance and new birth, in the kingdom of God.

It was not that Jesus' teachings were inapplicable to an entire society. According to Ulrich Stadler, Christ's commandments 'should constitute the polity of the whole world'. But the Anabaptists recognized that only those who had been reborn, and who were being sustained by the life of a family of faith, could obey these teachings. Hence their strategy. Let those who have become new creatures in Christ simply begin living in a new way now, in their relationships with each other. Let those men and women create churches of brothers and sisters, communities of faith, alternative forms of society in which the qualities which one day will characterize the kingdom of God will be prophetically present. In their practical, everyday living, let them realize the sharing of possessions, the love of brother/sister and enemy, and the openness and truthfulness of relationships which God intends for all his children.

The Anabaptists, it is thus clear, had a strong sense that the kingdom of God was among them. 'Christ, the Prince of Peace, has prepared and won for himself a Kingdom that is a Church,' exulted the Hutterite, Peter Riedemann. But the kingdom which had already come in their communal experience was for most people still in the future. Until God's rule was universal and uncontested, therefore, the Anabaptist congregations and communities must serve as signs, dramatizations, displays of what God intends for society.

The Anabaptists thus viewed each of their congregations simultaneously as a society for mission and an agency for social change. As their love for the Lord and each other grew, as their common life was transformed, they believed that the Holy Spirit would use Christ's life among them to invite others voluntarily to enter 'the Kingdom of Peace'.

In the course of time, the Anabaptist groupings lost this vision and vitality. Some lost it through toleration. The last execution in the northern Netherlands was in 1574. Soon thereafter the 'Baptism-minded' (as they came to call themselves) were finding a role in Dutch society as a respected, quasi-nonconformist subgroup whose members were especially prominent in medicine and the cloth trade. In other parts of Europe persecution lasted longer, and in time it led to exhaustion, legalism and withdrawal. For some of the Anabaptists' Mennonite descendants, William Penn in the late seventeenth century provided a haven in Pennsylvania. A century later Catherine the Great offered others of them toleration if they would introduce their farming methods into southern Russia. Migration and persecution, which had been the lot of the Anabaptists from the outset, have been experienced – somewhere in the world – by every subsequent generation of Mennonites.

In the 1980s, the spiritual descendants of the Anabaptists continue to exist; scattered across every continent, there are now some 670,000, slightly under half of whom live in Canada and the United States. Many of the surviving Anabaptist groups have recently experienced a renewing of their spirituality and vision, and are increasingly active in mission, service and inter-confessional dialogue. Some contemporaries, echoing the sixteenth-century Reformers, continue to dismiss the modern-day Anabaptists as ascetics who are 'superstitiously caught up in the small points'. Others, however, are more appreciative. Sensing themselves to be in a world that Christians can no longer control, they are finding in the Anabaptist tradition both theological insights and a living past.

Christian liberty

Robert Norris

In 1559, a number of clergymen returned to England from exile in Europe. They were members of the Church of England, who had taken refuge there to escape the persecution of Protestants in Queen Mary's reign. Mary had rejected the reformation of the church that had taken place under her father, Henry VIII. She wanted to restore the English church to the folds of Roman Catholicism, and to enforce her wishes she had burned those people who opposed her. With her death and the ascension to the throne of Elizabeth, a Protestant, many of the exiled clergy returned from their European refuges. They brought with them new patterns of belief which they had learned from their Continental friends, especially John Calvin in Geneva and Martin Bucer in Strasbourg. These emphases distinguished them from the rest of the clergy and became the earliest hallmarks of the Puritan movement.

The word Puritan means 'would-be reformer'; the returning exiles wanted to see the Church of England thoroughly reformed. Theologically, they would accept nothing as binding on the church that was not proved from the pages of Scripture. What was not demanded by the Bible could not be made mandatory on the conscience of an individual Christian without attacking the idea of Christian liberty.

Politically, the Puritans did not want the reformation of the church to be in the hands of the secular authorities. Instead, they demanded that the sole and final authority for the ordering of the church should be in the hands of the church's own officers.

Queen Elizabeth was sympathetic to the Protestant cause. Yet she was convinced that she herself must govern the church directly, because it was too powerful an institution to be left in hands that might not support her. And so she forced two Acts of Parliament to be passed. The first was the Act of Supremacy, which established the monarch as the head of the Church of England, and vested in her the power to rule and reform the church. The second was the Act of Uniformity, which required that all Englishmen should give religious obedience to the established Church of England. This obedience involved accepting the 'episcopal' form of government (bishops, priests and deacons) and also the set liturgical forms of worship.

The history of the Puritan protest movement falls into three periods, each period with specific demands for change, and each producing its own leaders:
● From Queen Elizabeth's ascension to the throne until the crushing of the Presbyterian movement in 1593;
● From the revival of the movement in 1593 until 1640, when the Long Parliament was called in Charles I's time;
● From 1640 through the period of Cromwell and Puritan ascendancy until 1660, with Charles II's return, the Restoration and the ejection of Puritan clergy from their positions.

The Puritans made an early impact on American history, through the Pilgrim Fathers, who were concerned to set up a

The quayside at Dartmouth, in Devonshire, England, where the Pilgrim Fathers put in aboard the Mayflower before crossing the Atlantic. The colony they established in Massachusetts was based on Puritan principles.

godly community under the rule of the Bible.

Not reformed enough

The initial principles of Puritanism were brought from Geneva and Zurich where the majority of the exiles had been given shelter. One of the first things they learned was to disdain the outward show of religion. On their return, the exiles found themselves in bitter opposition to the clergy wearing vestments, especially the surplice. But their objections were much more fundamental than simply refusing to dress up for church services. They were concerned that the reformation within the Church of England had not gone nearly far enough. As they saw it, Elizabeth was not prepared for a really thorough-going reform; she wanted only to preserve her own control of the church.

The University of Cambridge was the focal point of hostility to the Queen's policy, and it was from there, in 1570, that the first real Puritan leader emerged, with a distinct demand for change within the church. Thomas Cartwright was a young and very brilliant Professor of Divinity at the University. He delivered a series of lectures on the Book of Acts, in which he claimed that the Bible provided the outline for church government, and that this outline was better expressed in Presbyterian church government than by the system of bishops.

Cartwright called for bishops to be abolished and for a form of church order to be set up based more on laypeople. He wanted to establish the kingdom of God on earth, and in England. The church was to be independent of the control of rulers: it would be related to the government, but not controlled by it. The first task of the church was to call people to obey God; only then should they be taught their duty to the state. He firmly maintained that we are all sinners, and that secular power, whoever holds it, is purely a gift from God. Within the church, anybody with the spiritual quality, regardless of social position, can be chosen to teach and serve. Along with this, he advocated the Presbyterian idea of church democracy: every congregation should have the right to elect its own elders and ministers, and the national church should be maintained by a series of representative assemblies, at different levels, composed both of clergymen and laypeople.

Cartwright was dismissed from his position of Professor of Divinity at Cambridge by Archbishop Whitgift, who was a firm supporter of the royal control of the church. The archbishop saw in the scheme not only that bishops would have a less important role, but also that the monarch would be less able to control the church's policy and life.

Cartwright continued to write and lecture. He gained a great following within the established church, but yet none of the reforms he so badly wanted actually came to fruition. This was partly due to a division within the Puritan party itself.

One group rejected the idea that the Presbyterian system was taught in the New Testament. They found in the Bible that each local church was vested with the absolute power to determine its own course of action and its own destiny. They also thought unbiblical the idea of a mixed church, combining devoted Christian people with purely nominal attenders. They wanted to restrict membership of the church to the clearly committed. This approach, often called 'Independency', is close to the Anabaptist policy, described in *God's left wing*. It went against the whole idea of a national or established church to which all members of the nation belonged, and at the same time it imposed a threat to the power that the monarch could influence within the church. It certainly would have reduced the political importance of the church, and the crown would no longer have been able to use the church to affect the life of the people.

Because of this division within his own supporters, Cartwright could not put together a unified opposition to the episcopal structure of the Church of England. He was frustrated not only by those who held independent views, but also by those who, while holding the general spiritual principles of Puritanism, remained loyal to the Church of England and would have no part in the specific demands for reform. With Cartwright dismissed and his attempts to effect a Presbyterian order of church government aborted, the first phase of the Puritan movement was completed.

Making the Bible understood

The group who remained loyal to the Church of England while accepting Cartwright's spiritual leadership included one outstanding figure – William Perkins. He was destined to be one of the most popular and influential of the Puritan leaders. His intellectual achievements in theology gave the movement widespread credibility, and his emphasis on the Christian's personal devotion became one of the hallmarks of Puritanism.

Perkins had been educated at Christ's College, Cambridge and had come under the influence of the developing Puritan movement. He was in favour of much of Cartwright's spiritual teaching, but he rejected his scheme of church government. Like him, he was concerned for an educated ministry. All too often, churches found themselves under the ministry of the youngest sons of nobles, who saw the system of patronage within the church as a lucrative and easy path to advancement. Sometimes these men knew so little that they hired others to say services for them, and the worship became unintelligible.

Again, Perkins recognized the prime place of preaching within worship, and this was another Puritan emphasis. Over many years, preaching had ceased to play a significant part in the church's worship. All sorts of rituals and ceremonies had been introduced, so that many of the services contained little or no teaching. Perkins, in common with most Puritans, realized the importance of educating the congregations in the truths of the Bible. The Puritans believed that the Bible contained the perfect rule for living, believing and worshipping, and so they strove to make its teaching as widely known and understood as possible. Preaching was seen to be God's way of educating the people and changing the church.

Perkins had the same beliefs as all Puritans. They were basically those set out by John Calvin in his *Institutes of the Christian Religion*, (see *Life-bringers*). God is sovereign in everything, and people can only find the forgiveness they need through the death of Jesus Christ reconciling them to God.

Together with this intellectual framework, Perkins had the Puritan longing for simplicity in worship, uncluttered by ceremony or ritual. Because of this, there were two attempts to have him removed from his position and ejected from the Church of England. Yet his clear loyalty to the established church, together with the support of some of his influential friends, protected him from being seriously threatened.

His early death in 1602, at the age of forty-four, robbed Puritanism of one of its most influential advocates. He was

respected as a prominent churchman, was a popular apologist for Protestantism against Roman Catholicism, and had wide influence through his writings. In these writings he stressed something which was to become one of the key points of Puritan spirituality. Until Perkins, dogmatic or systematic theology had been seen as the major task of a theologian. But he brought a vision of applying the Calvinist system of belief to practical questions. His aim was no less than to make Christian truth relate to people's lives as well as their minds.

No bishop, no king

When Elizabeth died in 1603, she was succeeded by James VI of Scotland, who had been brought up in a Presbyterian church with a strict discipline, aware of Calvinist theology. The Puritans gained a new hope. Would this new king make their dream of reform a reality?

While on his way to claim the throne, James was met by a delegation of Puritans and asked to reform the church. He agreed to meet with Puritan representatives at a later date, and a meeting was eventually held at Hampton Court Palace. At the conference, the Puritans presented to the King a list of obvious reforms that they felt should be implemented to bring the church in line with the Bible. Their list included the abolition of the bishops, and the restructuring of the church along Presbyterian lines.

The Puritans were great preachers, applying Bible teaching to their times. This tradition still has many followers worldwide.

John Knox was the leading Reformer in Scotland. He sternly denounced all forms of idolatry, and taught that it was legitimate to oppose idolatrous monarchs. The Puritans found him a more acceptable model than some of the English Reformers.

This reminded James of experiences he wanted to forget. He had grown up with the democratic Presbyterianism of Scotland's John Knox, where the preacher could rebuke the King in public. This made him determined that, as Ruler of England, he would control the church and never again be subject to the discipline of ministers. He had also come to believe that government by bishops was a means of maintaining the position of the monarch as the supreme earthly governor of the church – a position to which James believed himself divinely appointed. This is why James said to the assembled Puritans his famous 'no bishops, no king', and tied himself to the traditional episcopal government of the church. Instead of the debate and reform they hoped for, the Puritan party received a crushing blow. They were to be ordered to conform to the King's wish. In fact, the only one of their proposals that the King accepted, was for a new translation of the Bible in the English language. This gained approval and the Authorized, 'King James' Version of the Bible came into being in 1611.

James had become afraid of the growing influence of the Puritans and was determined to drive them out of the church. He deprived them of their livings and, unlike Elizabeth, refused to tolerate their existence within the established church. Although he agreed with them theologically, and even wrote some theological books with a Calvinist position, he was determined to prevent the creation of a church which could in any way challenge the power of the crown.

The agent of persecution was Archbishop Laud, a man whose strong 'high church' position had caused many to accuse him of secret sympathy with the Roman Catholic Church. Laud is supposed to have had a list drawn up of all the clergymen in England. Against each of the names he allegedly placed either a P or an O – Puritan or Orthodox. He then began to try and drive the Puritans from their churches.

At the same time as attacking the Puritan clergy, James and Laud determined to reduce some of the power of the nobility and to frustrate the growing call for democratic rule. Many of the emerging middle class and some nobles joined the Puritan movement as a vehicle for their political opposition to James and the policies of Laud.

The Puritans were driven underground. They began to preach a strong gospel, directing their calls for reform no longer towards the ruler, but to any or all of the people of God. The preachers fired the people's political will. People who were searching for salvation should not only trust in Jesus Christ, but also put on the whole armour of God. They preached a gospel which called for strength and action as well as faith. God's kingdom would only be established in the face of hostility and opposition, and this required strength and discipline and courage. The goal was a land where the authority of the Bible would be paramount, and where the Bible's teaching would be the legal and moral basis for national life.

Civil war

By 1610, much of the opposition to the policies of James' house of Stuart found a rallying point in political Puritanism. Within one generation this hostility was to break out in civil war – a war in which the supporters of royal privilege were found opposed to the growing democratic party, whose leadership was solidly Puritan.

The period between James coming to the throne and the eventual triumph of the Puritan party saw the rise of two famous leaders whose names have become synonymous with Puritanism: John Owen and Richard Baxter.

Owen was born and educated in the climate of political and theological controversy created by Stuart policies. He was a staunch supporter of the rights of a democratic Parliament over and against the royal supremacy. He was also an Independent in church government, demanding the right of the local congregation to elect its own leaders and to be accountable to God alone under the Bible. Owen was also a rigid Calvinist in his theological position, and this at a time when the leaders of the Church of England under Laud were quite the opposite – liturgical and idealistic in practice, anti-Calvinist in theology.

Eventually, the rift between Charles and his Parliament became an open civil war, with the vast majority of the Puritan party ranged against the King. Owen became one of the chaplains to the Parliamentary Army and in this capacity exercised great influence and travelled extensively. With the defeat of the King and his eventual execution, the 'Long Parliament', with its Puritan bias, ruled the country. Among its first acts was one to abolish the Church of England as an episcopal church – no more

Oliver Cromwell, Lord Protector of England in the seventeenth-century, was a Puritan through and through. The time of his leadership saw the ascendancy of Puritan teaching and policies.

bishops. This meant that a Parliamentary Committee had to be set up to validate the ordination of those who presented themselves for ministry within churches, and to oversee the transfer of clergy from one church to another.

Owen was not included in this structure, nor was he invited to be a member of the Westminster Assembly of Divines which was convened to produce an alternative basis of faith to the 39 Articles of the old Church of England. The reason for his exclusion was that he held very firm Independent views, while Parliament was inclined to Presbyterian thought, confirmed by the help the Scots and their Presbyterian army had given in the Civil War.

However, with the growth of Oliver Cromwell's power, there came an increase in the influence of the Independents, and not least John Owen. Eventually the Long

The state of Pennsylvania was founded by the Quaker William Penn – the name is literally 'Penn's Woods'. New England Puritanism was therefore not the only Christian influence in early America. But nonconformity was the strongest common factor, and this helped imprint on American character and institutions a strong belief in individual liberty of conscience and independence from state control.

Parliament was dismissed and Cromwell assumed the rule of the nation as the Lord Protector. Owen was made Chancellor of the University of Oxford, where his outstanding theological intellect earned him an international reputation. At the same time, his influence in matters of government increased, and he is in no small part responsible for the failure to introduce a Presbyterian order to the national church. His belief in Congregationalism, allied to Cromwell's power, thwarted the Scots' desire to impose the Presbyterian order.

Owen fell from favour with Cromwell when he opposed the Protector's wish to become King. Yet he remained one of the most influential of the Puritans until the time of his death. Even under Charles II, his reputation and personal qualities saved him from the persecution which fell on so many others. His stature as thinker and political preacher, his integrity as an honourable man, helped make him one of the most outstanding of Puritans.

Richard Baxter, the other great figure of this period, was a gentle man and a scholar, chiefly famous for his pastoral theology encapsulated in *The Reformed Pastor* – a

study in the personal piety and calling of the Christian minister. As one of the leaders of religious thought and devotion, Baxter was concerned about the whole pastoral state of the church. While ministering at Kidderminster, he worked to produce the theory and practice which made for Christian godliness. At the same time, he emphasized the importance of Christian unity in an age which saw more virtue in separation. His works all display a warmth that is not always one of the marks of the Puritan movement.

A spiritual battle

The history of the Puritans is a history of their spirituality. It is this that linked the generations. The source of their faith, and the guide of their worship and conduct, was the Bible. They lived under the conviction that Jesus Christ spoke through the Bible, and so its authority was paramount. They were also very careful to encourage personal reading of the Scriptures. The high water mark of English Puritanism under Oliver Cromwell saw the publication of large numbers of manuals to aid in the correct interpretation of the Bible and to provoke spiritual self-examination.

The Pilgrim Fathers give thanks to God for their first harvest after landing at Plymouth, Massachusetts. This is the origin of Thanksgiving Day. Americans look back to those early Christian settlers as an example of courage and faith. Ever since then Protestant Christianity has been a vitally important part of American national life.

Puritan literature abounds with spiritual biographies, full of detailed accounts of struggles with Satan. The concept of spiritual warfare became a central theme of the movement. The goal of the Christian life was to persevere to the last in the face of demonic attack. Large numbers of books of advice for living the Christian life were produced. This literature had a threefold emphasis: strictness of discipline, desire for personal holiness, and strong personal devotion to Christ.

These spiritual principles were the great strength of Puritanism. There were also weaknesses, and these have been woven into the caricature that remains with us. The rigidity of thought and lifestyle made the Puritans appear legalistic. History has remembered that under their rule, following the execution of Charles I, England was forced to adopt laws that legislated for public and private morality. They restricted people's private liberty and forced them grimly to accept a joyless morality.

The moralism which resulted from much of the Puritan legislation was a direct result of trying to usher in the kingdom of God by Act of Parliament. They banned public dancing, they apparently destroyed everything of aesthetic quality. And this has left a distorted picture of what Puritanism really was.

While it is true that many Puritans were excessive in their search for innocent pleasures to attack, Butler's picture of them as 'low born, sour-faced hypocrites jealously disapproving the pleasures of their superiors' is a misrepresentation. They were lovers of art as distinct from what they saw as idolatry. They encouraged music and produced and acclaimed John Milton. Economic life within the nation was restored, because they accepted the Bible's work ethic and put it into practice. They showed courage in adversity and held to principle in the face of personal loss and danger, and these were among the characteristics of the dedicated, God-fearing, disciplined and moral society that Puritanism produced.

The Puritan legacy

Through the Pilgrim Fathers, the Puritan way of Christian liberty has had an impact on the American approach to life and faith. The Pilgrims dreamt of founding a colony that would be an example to England of God's kingdom on earth. Their dream embodied all that was best of Puritanism and yet also the seeds of the worst excesses. Under John Winthrop, the highest ideals of personal piety and communal support were given life. The Pilgrims were intellectual, biblical, tolerant at first, democratic and peace-loving – qualities severely tested in dealing with native Americans, with debt, sickness and starvation. They were among the first groups to practise inter-communion with other Christian groups. Yet the seeds of division and bigotry were also present. These seeds were to lead to a history of separation and heresy-hunting that turned the Puritan dream into a nightmare.

The impact of Puritanism remains. In England, with the restoration of Charles II, the Puritans were ejected from their churches, and forbidden to meet. This gave the impetus to the different elements to form their own denominations. We may trace the rise of the modern free churches from this time. The denominations enshrined many of the Puritan emphases of discipline and practical spirituality. And yet the heart of the Puritan longing never came to fruition. The idea of a fully Reformed National Church, which had been the binding agent and the driving force of the movement, was lost on both sides of the Atlantic.

John Milton, the leading poet of his age, was a strong Puritan. His example gives the lie to the idea that the Puritans were totally against all cultural activity. But their main social emphases were on work and on principle in political life.

Strangely warmed

A. Skevington Wood

The University of Oxford has strong associations with the beginnings of the 'Methodist revival'. Here the famous Holy Club met, its members looking for a depth of spiritual life not often found in the England of their time.

The scene is set in the city of Oxford, England. It is a warm Sunday afternoon in June. The year is 1738.

As the clock in the famous Tom Tower strikes two, an impressive procession moves slowly into the university church of St Mary the Virgin on High Street. It is led by an official bearing the insignia of the Vice-Chancellor, followed by the Vice-Chancellor himself arrayed in all his finery. Sandwiched between him and the university Proctors is the select preacher for the day, with the scarlet-robed Doctors of Divinity bringing up the rear.

This is a university service which all resident members are expected to attend. The church fills as a hymn is sung and a bidding prayer offered. Then the preacher, small in stature and quiet in manner, announces his text from Ephesians 2:8 – 'By grace are ye saved through faith'.

Before long it is clear that this is no routine sermon. It is a cry from the heart and a call to battle. It is the manifesto of a new movement within the church of God.

It heralds the advent of what became known as 'the Methodist revival'.

The preacher was John Wesley, almost thirty-five years of age, the son of a cleric and a Fellow of Lincoln College in Oxford. The message was a re-affirmation of the Protestant Reformers' emphasis on free grace and saving faith. Nothing but this, Wesley declared, could check the immorality which was flooding the land. Endeavouring to empty 'the ocean of wickedness' drop by drop through piecemeal reforms was a futile exercise. Only the proclamation of the 'righteousness which is of God by faith' could stem the tide of permissiveness.

In such direct and uncompromising

terms Wesley threw down his challenge. It was more than enough to disturb the customary calm of a Sunday afternoon university service. It represented the opening salvo of a campaign which was to cover the whole of England and eventually spread far beyond it.

John Wesley's own days as a don at Lincoln College, Oxford had ended in 1735 but, while there, his rooms had been the rendezvous for the so-called 'Holy Club', formed in 1729. This dedicated group of tutors, graduates and undergraduates— never more than some twenty in number— combined prayer, fasting and Bible study with visits to the sick, the poor and those in prison. The members may have been strangers to the experience of Christian conversion at the time, but their commitment to each other and to those they tried to help was exemplary. Even after Wesley's departure from Oxford the group continued to function and, indeed, to extend its influence.

Between 1735 and 1738, the Wesley brothers, John and Charles, undertook a mission to the Indians and colonists in Georgia, which proved a fiasco. On his return to England, John Wesley wrote, 'I went to America to convert the Indians, but, oh, who shall convert me?' Yet the

John Wesley's ministry in Britain was both long in duration and widespread in effect. He travelled prodigiously and preached wherever there was opportunity. By the time his work ended, the social life of the nation was at a higher moral level than it had been a few decades before.

One great feature of Methodism has always been hymn singing. Charles Wesley wrote a great many hymns to popular tunes. Hymn singing has been a main part of Christian worship since that time.

university service in June 1738 saw him preaching with new-found conviction and issuing an epoch-making appeal to a decadent nation. What had made the difference?

Turning-point

The most significant fact was that only eighteen days before preaching this sermon, Wesley had experienced an

evangelical conversion. His heart had been 'strangely warmed', as he put it, at a little meeting in Aldersgate Street, London, where someone read from Martin Luther's preface to Paul's letter to the Romans. The passage describes the nature of faith – the faith that brings a man into a right relationship with God. Wesley had already accepted the doctrine of justification by faith with his mind. Now, under the instruction of his Moravian friend, Peter Böhler, he began to seek the reality of it for himself. On 24 May 1738, he became truly aware of it for the first time, and received an assurance that the death of Jesus Christ had indeed freed him from the punishment he deserved for his sin.

Up to this turning-point, Wesley had been a sort of spiritual Hamlet. An Anglican clergyman for many years, he was still unsure of his vocation. He now knew that his salvation had been dearly bought, and he felt that he must endeavour to repay the mighty debt he owed by devoting his life to spreading this good news. It was the 'warmed heart' which made Wesley an evangelist. The flame lit in Aldersgate Street was the real beginning of his God-given mission.

CHRIST IN HIS CHURCH
Michael Harper

In 1833 the English prime minister warned the country's bishops 'to set their house in order'. Though he did not complete the quotation from the Old Testament book of Kings, others did: 'for thou shalt die'. A mob in Bristol burned down the bishop's residence, and Dr Arnold, headmaster of Rugby School, wrote, 'the church as it now stands, no human power can save'. Some years earlier in London, only six people had attended Easter Communion in St Paul's Cathedral.

The Church of England was ripe for a new movement, and in 1833 she got it; the leaders were to be called – as well as other things less compli-mentary – 'Tractarians'.

Beginnings

In July 1833 John Keble, a Fellow of Oriel College, Oxford, preached the annual assize sermon. He called it 'National Apostasy', and particularly attacked a Bill before parliament to make half the Irish bishops redundant. Those present can have had little idea that the sermon heralded a movement which was to have a revolutionary effect on church life in Britain.

Ten days after the assize sermon, four men met at Hadleigh Rectory in Suffolk to make proposals for action. John Keble, undoubtedly the founder of what became known as the Oxford Movement, was not among them. But one of his disciples – Richard Froude – was. In the short time before his death three years later, Froude did something which was to be crucial in the development of the Movement. He converted a young Fellow of Oriel College from evangelical to high church views. His name was John Henry Newman, and he was to

become the Oxford Movement's most famous leader, ultimately joining the Roman Catholic Church and becoming a cardinal.

The four who met at Hadleigh took an important decision: to issue some pamphlets which they called *Tracts for the Times* (hence the name Tractarians). These were anonymously-written, four-page leaflets and sold for a penny each. Newman cycled round the villages of Oxfordshire with bundles of these tracts, selling them wherever he could to the local clergy. An early member of the group was a young politician called William Gladstone, who later became one of Britain's finest prime ministers.

The Oxford Movement spread throughout Britain. For the first three years, it caused no apparent trouble. But the lull ended in 1836 and a storm of persecution began which was to last many years. The Tractarians were accused of popery and dubbed 'Puseyites' (after Edward Pusey, the noted

Methodism as a movement sprang from the conversion of John Wesley, and that of his brother Charles three days beforehand. At the same time, the central message of the Methodist revival was determined. 'Salvation by grace through faith' became Wesley's 'standing topic', shared by all who were his partners in preaching the gospel. His ministry was revolutionized by his recognition of this fundamental principle: that we are forgiven and made right with God on the basis of what Jesus' death and resurrection achieved, not because of our own merit or effort.

It would be hard to overestimate the impact of this one man on the age in which he lived. Other figures – especially that of George Whitefield – were undoubtedly prominent, but measured by the mark he made on England as a whole, Wesley stands above the rest. The poet Robert Southey considered him to be 'the most influential mind of the eighteenth century'. A more recent writer regards him as 'the ascendant personality' of the period. His aim was 'to reform the nation' and, by the time he died in 1791, the movement he led had made an impression for good not only on thousands of individual men and women but also on English society in general, and not least the Church of England which at first resisted his message.

As the essayist Augustine Birrell graphically expressed it, Wesley 'contested three kingdoms in the cause of Christ, during a campaign which lasted fifty years'. He travelled, mostly on horseback, close on a quarter of a million miles, or the equivalent of nine times round the earth. He reached more people with the good news of Jesus Christ than anyone before him in the British Isles, and set forces in motion which have not lost their momentum to this day.

'The great awakener'

The origins of the Methodist movement, however, and its expression in the Evangelical Awakening of which it was a part, are to be sought further back than the conversion of the Wesleys. George Whitefield was a leader of virtually comparable importance – especially in the early days of the revival.

In many ways Whitefield was the pioneer. It was he who first preached on the need for 'the new birth' as the means of entering God's kingdom. It was he who

---

Oxford academic who joined the group in 1834). This was untrue – at least in its early stages the Oxford Movement was anti-Catholic. The blurb on the first tracts professed them to be 'against Popery and dissent'. Dr Arnold led the first assault, to be followed by other leaders; the Bishop of Chester called the Movement 'a work of Satan'.

Newman's *Tract 90*, written in 1841, provoked a storm of abuse. In it he attempted to show that the Anglican Thirty-Nine Articles were not against the Roman Catholic Church and could be interpreted in a Catholic sense. At the same time, Newman himself began to have doubts about Anglican orthodoxy, and in 1842 he retired from all office in the Church of England. In 1845 he was received into 'the one Fold of Christ', as he called the Church of Rome.

A fresh start

To some, Newman's departure seemed to mark the end of the Oxford Movement; but instead it transformed it into a new power. Contrary to expectations, none of the other leaders followed suit.

The Movement had reflected far too much the views of Newman. Other men now became involved and its nerve-centre moved away from Oxford. Persecution continued, and Queen Victoria saw to it that no honours or promotion fell to the Tractarians. John Keble, the founder, died in 1866 without honours, although later he had an Oxford College named after him.

The Tractarians possessed superb leaders, men of saintliness as well as learning. In Newman, and later in Henry Liddon, they possessed two of the best preachers in Britain. Tractarian hymns (especially those by F. W. Faber, J. M. Neale and Newman himself) matched those of the Wesleys. Later in Sir Gilbert Scott and William Butterfield they produced architects; James Mozley and Edward Pusey were theologians of the highest calibre. They restored religious communities within the Anglican Church, renewed worship (they introduced choirs), emphasized the importance of holy communion and later pioneered social action. They were also the first to be concerned about conditions in the inner cities.

If it could be said that the evangelicals saved the Church of England at the end of the eighteenth century, the same could be claimed for the Tractarians in the nineteenth. They have left their mark permanently on the church scene.

first recognized the urgency of evangelizing on 'the aggressive system'. It was he who first saw large-scale conversions to Christ. It was he who first employed lay preachers. Much that Wesley was to exploit with such success had been initiated by Whitefield.

Whitefield's conversion to Christ preceded that of the Wesley brothers by some three years. Little is known of the circumstances, except that it was while he was up at Oxford and a member of the group nicknamed the Holy Club. Whitefield evidently passed through what the mystics call 'the dark night of the soul', culminating in a prostrating illness, before 'a full assurance of faith broke in on his disconsolate soul.' He himself described his Christian experience as 'the day of my espousals, – a day to be had in everlasting remembrance. At first my joys were like a spring tide and, as it were, overflowed the banks; afterwards it became more settled – and, blessed be God, saving a few casual intervals, has abode and increased in my soul ever since.'

Not for nothing has George Whitefield been dubbed 'the great awakener'. His own spiritual 'awakening' in 1735 prepared him for his distinctive ministry.

In the fewer years that were spared to him, Whitefield was as prodigal as Wesley in his efforts to spread the message of

Hogarth's cartoon 'Gin Lane' shows some of the background to the Wesleys' England. It was a society in need of moral and spiritual renewal. John Wesley believed in going, not just to those who needed him, but to those who needed him most.

THE LORD'S WATCH

A. Skevington Wood

As its name suggests, the Moravian movement originated in Moravia, a province in present-day Czechoslavakia. At first an independent state, Moravia was taken into Bohemia under the flag of the German Empire in 1029. And it was in Bohemia that Jan Hus, one of the 'pre-Reformation reformers', led resistance to the Church of Rome and was finally martyred in 1415.

After his heroic death, a group who maintained his beliefs eventually formed a New Testament community at Kunwald. In 1457 they established what they called 'The Church of the Brotherhood'. They were subsequently joined by others of similar outlook and their title then became *Unitas Fratrum* (The Unity of the Brethren) or, more usually, the Moravians.

Their numbers grew so rapidly that by the early seventeenth century it was claimed that more than half the Protestant population of Europe had been won over to them. When the Bohemians were defeated soon after the outbreak of the Thirty Years' War, many of the Moravians had to run for their lives. They were scattered all over Europe and some abandoned their faith. But a few held together, even in Bohemia – the 'hidden seed' for whom the first Moravian bishop, Jan Amos Comenius, prayed so fervently while exiled in Poland.

His faith was to be vindicated in a most exciting fashion.

In 1715 there were signs of spiritual revival in Bohemia – both at Fulnek (where Comenius had ministered) and at Lititz. Then in 1722 two families named Neisser, led by Christian David (known as 'the servant of the Lord'), left Bohemia for a settlement in Saxony provided for them by a Lutheran nobleman, Count Nikolaus of Zinzendorf. He placed his estate at Bertheldsdorf at their disposal. In the next seven years some 300 Protestant refugees made their way to this haven from all parts of Germany, as well as from Bohemia and Moravia.

A community similar to the original one at Kunwald grew up. As Christian David felled a tree on the site with his carpenter's axe, he repeated the words of the psalmist: 'Even the sparrow has found a home, and the swallow a nest for herself – even your altars, O Lord of hosts.' The plot of land was situated on the Hutberg or Watch Hill, so the place was renamed Herrnhut – 'the Lord's Watch'. Johann Andreas Rothe was installed as pastor in the Lutheran church at Bertheldsdorf.

Renewal

It was in 1727 that the community had a most remarkable experience of God's Holy Spirit, which prepared the Moravians for the crucial part they were to play in the Methodist revival. At a Sunday afternoon communion service, they were made aware of God's renewing power to such an extent that, according to one account, they left 'hardly knowing whether they belonged to earth or had already gone to heaven'.

The effects of this transforming experience were widespread. Zinzendorf himself abandoned his legal career to superintend the movement. The Moravians were to become the pioneer missionaries of the eighteenth century and prove a major influence in the Evangelical Awakening in England. Their worldwide evangelistic enterprise was soon launched and deserves an honoured place in the saga of modern missionary expansion.

In 1732 Leonard Dober and David Nitschmann began a work on the island of St Thomas in the Caribbean, and from that date onwards the range of Moravian missionary activity was extended to include other areas in the West Indies, North America,

Greenland, Lapland, many parts of the South American and African continents, Persia (now Iran), India, Ceylon (Sri Lanka), the East Indies (Indonesia) and Australia. Considering the hazards of sea travel at the time, as well as the threats to health involved, the record is nothing short of heroic!

The Moravian impact on the evangelical revival in England was twofold. It was through meeting Moravian leaders such as August Spangenberg and Peter Böhler that John and Charles Wesley came to a full understanding of the gospel and experienced true conversion. But beyond that, from 1738 onwards, Moravians were intensely active in efforts to evangelize the whole of the nation. Starting in London itself, this initiative quickly spread to other areas. Yorkshire was to become a stronghold under Benjamin Ingham, while John Cennick, after fruitful missions in Wiltshire, spearheaded the campaign in Ireland.

The Moravians were the great missionaries of their time. In many respects they were the spearhead of what was to become the modern missionary movement.

Coalminers today do a hard and sometimes dangerous job. But for their counterparts in eighteenth-century England, life was immeasurably worse, placing them among the most needy groups in society. When George Whitefield preached to the miners at Kingswood, near Bristol, he expected a tough reception. But the men were deeply moved and asked him to come back and preach again.

salvation and forgiveness. 'I had rather wear out than rust out,' he said. 'A true faith in Jesus Christ will not suffer us to be idle. No; it is an active, lively, restless principle; it fills the heart so that it cannot be easy till it is doing something for Jesus Christ.' Whitefield preached on average for up to sixty hours a week. He reached almost every corner of England and Wales, went to Scotland fifteen times and Ireland twice, and paid no less than seven visits to North America. His expressed wish was that he could 'fly from pole to pole preaching the everlasting gospel!'

One of his biographers described Whitefield as a 'wayfaring witness' and so he was. As a preacher and an evangelist he was without equal in effectiveness. Although he and the Wesleys were to part company after a difference of theological opinion, they never lost their regard for each other, and no account of the Methodist movement is complete without recognizing the part played by Whitefield in its birth and growth.

The 'state of the nation'

What, then, were the conditions in eighteenth-century England and its established church which called for urgent reform and renewal?

There can be no serious doubt that moral standards and behaviour had declined alarmingly. The Church of England was poorly equipped to deal with the situation, and the nonconformists were in no better shape. Nothing short of a spiritual awakening could meet the desperate need of the hour.

John Wesley himself painted a devastating picture: 'Is there a nation under the sun, which is so deeply fallen from the very first principles of all religion? Where is the country in which is found so utter a disregard to even heathen morality, such a thorough contempt of justice and truth, and all that should be dear and honourable to rational creatures? . . . Such a complication of villainies of every kind, considered with all their aggravations, such a scorn of whatever bears the face of virtue, such injustice, fraud and falsehood; above all, such perjury, and such a method of law, we may defy the whole world to produce.'

There is ample evidence to indicate that such a trenchant indictment was no exaggeration. With 253 capital offences on the statute-book, the law had fallen into disrepute and in many cases could not be put into effect. Anarchy and violence prevailed. The nickname 'Sir Mob' was an acknowledgement of the strength of mob rule in the cities. No-go areas were not unusual. Footpads and pickpockets abounded. Shoplifting was on the increase. Muggings were an everyday occurrence. Gambling reached epidemic proportions.

Drunkenness amounted to a national disgrace. The gin craze had so enslaved the populace that novelist Henry Fielding, in his capacity as a London magistrate, declared that 'should the drinking of this poison be continued at its present height during the next twenty years, there will, by that time, be very few of the common people left to drink it'.

Cruel and degrading 'sports' – such as bear-baiting, bull-baiting, badger-baiting, cock-fighting, goose-riding, dog-tailing – reflected the brutal temper of the age. Prize fights with the minimum of protective rules attracted large crowds. Sometimes the contestants were women: one known as 'Bruising Peg' was a champion.

The licentiousness of the eighteenth-century stage was deplored by Joseph Addison in the pages of *The Spectator* and conceded even by 'a man of the world' like Lord Hervey in his memoirs. No wonder Wesley castigated the theatre as 'that sink of all profaneness and debauchery'.

This landslide into permissiveness was rightly seen by the spiritually alert as stemming from an abandonment of living, Christian faith. The denial of God had resulted in a ditching of moral sanctions. Thomas Secker, then Bishop of Oxford, recognized the connection between the two when he referred to 'this unhappy age of irreligion and libertinism'. Sir John Barnard, an outstanding MP of the time,

The Wesley Chapel in London was a centre of early Methodism.

regretted that 'at present it really seems to
be the fashion for a man to declare himself
of no religion', and hymn-writer Isaac
Watts called on Christians to 'use all just
and proper efforts for the recovery of dying
religion'.

Theologically the church seemed to be
exhausted by its struggle with the Deists,
who did not believe that God had revealed
himself directly to mankind. In too many
instances, Deism had gained the upper
hand. Many younger laymen succumbed to
this philosophy, and defection was not
unknown among the ranks of the clergy. At
the same time, there had been a dramatic
drop in the sale of Christian books.
Sermons in church had degenerated into
lifeless moral exhortations, inviting hearers
to do good and to be good without really
showing them how. It has been said that
they fell into three categories – dull, duller
and dullest!

Quite obviously there must have been
exceptions to this powerless and
demoralized picture. Some of the religious
societies set up in the mid-seventeenth
century as safeguards against
permissiveness continued to flourish
throughout this period. Yet, when every
allowance has been made for such
mitigating factors, there can be no question
about the general impotence of the
institutional church to arrest the moral and
spiritual collapse of the nation.

Fire of revival

This appalling decline had brought both
church and state to the brink of catastrophe
when God intervened in revival. In the
words of Wesley himself, 'just at this time
. . . two or three clergymen of the Church of
England began vehemently to "call sinners
to repentance". In two or three years they
had sounded the alarm to the utmost
borders of the land. Many thousands
gathered to hear them; and in every place
where they came, many began to show
such concern for religion as they had never
done before.'

The awakening, Wesley later recorded,
dated from the year 1738. 'Then it pleased
God to kindle a fire which I trust shall
never be extinguished.'

John Wesley's conversion, along with
that of his brother Charles, was a critical
turning-point in the initiation of the
Methodist movement. It was this change
which made him into 'the apostle of
England'. The sermon in St Mary's, Oxford,
less than three weeks later, represented the

first trumpet-blast of a reforming crusade.

But it was at a remarkable gathering on New Year's Day, 1739, that the leaders of the movement had a sudden and memorable experience of God's Holy Spirit. From then onwards, Methodism was more than a programme for reform. It was caught up in a wave of revival in which the dynamic for mission was supplied by God himself through the Holy Spirit.

On Monday 1 January 1739, the Wesleys and Whitefield, together with members of the Holy Club and about sixty others, met for a 'love feast', or *agape*. This communal fellowship meal was a feature of the life of the early Christian church revived by the Moravians.

The room where they gathered was in Fetter Lane, London, where what is regarded as the first Methodist society now regularly assembled. Whitefield described this occasion as 'the happiest New Year's Day that I ever yet saw'. God supported him without sleep, and the whole night was spent in 'close prayer, psalms and thanksgivings'.

John Wesley now takes up the tale. 'About three in the morning, as we were continuing instant in prayer, the power of God came mightily upon us, in so much that many cried out for exceeding joy, and many fell to the ground. As soon as we were recovered a little from that awe and amazement at the presence of his majesty we broke out with one voice, "We praise thee, O God; we acknowledge thee to be the Lord".'

This 'Pentecost at New Year' proved to be the launching-pad for the Methodist mission. It was the prelude to a period of swift and striking church growth and a sustained assault on the forces of evil in the land.

Out in the open

The Methodist movement now had its men and its message. The inherited concept of a religious society was to provide the means for nurturing new Christian converts and establishing believers in their faith. What was now needed was a method by which 'the masses' could be reached, since so few of them ever attended a church. Such a method was discovered almost inadvertently and by the pressure of circumstances. It was nevertheless to supply the missing link in the evangelistic strategy of Methodism.

It all came about early in 1739, when

George Whitefield ran into difficulties as he left London hoping to preach in Bath and Bristol. The opposition he had already encountered in England's capital was now displayed in the West Country too. After being refused two churches, he appealed to the chancellor of the diocese who put an embargo on him, even forbidding him to preach in the prisons.

Whitefield, however, was convinced that he had a message from God to deliver. He remembered that Jesus spoke to the crowds who flocked to hear him on the mountain-side or down by the lake. Whitefield's attention was drawn to the Kingswood coal-miners – a rough, sullen, often vicious set of men who lived and worked in appalling conditions. Women and even children joined them underground, toiling for long hours in the dust and dirt of the coal-mines, exposed to danger and disease.

It was to these victims of an unjust social system that Whitefield's heart went out in compassion, with the result that on 17 February 1739, he ventured to preach the gospel message to them out of doors. Some 200 were present on that first occasion, but there were 2,000 the second time, and before long the numbers shot up to 10,000 and even 20,000. 'Blessed be God that I have now broken the ice!' Whitefield wrote in his *Journal*. 'I believe I was never more acceptable to my Master than when I was standing to teach those hearers in the open fields. Some may censure me, but if I thus pleased men I should not be the servant of Christ.'

Although there were those who thought it improper for a clergyman to demean himself by appearing before the lower classes in this fashion, Whitefield knew that he had a commission to fulfil. From that time on, he declared, 'field preaching is my plan.' He was now convinced that 'mounts are the best pulpits, and the heavens the best sounding-boards'. Back in London, he was not allowed to preach in St Mary's, Islington, and so resorted to the churchyard to give his message there. Soon he was offering new life in Christ in Moorfields, 'the city Mall', on Kennington Common and Hampstead Heath, in Hyde Park, Smithfields, Mayfair . . .

'Blessed be God!' he cried, 'we begin to surround this great city!' As Spurgeon once observed, it was a brave day for England when Whitefield began to preach in the open.

John Wesley was soon to follow in his steps. He was more than a little reluctant to begin with: 'I could scarce reconcile myself at first to this strange way of preaching in the fields . . . having been all my life (till very lately) so tenacious of every point relating to decency and order, that I should have thought the saving of souls almost a sin if it had not been done in a church.' But he 'submitted to be more vile' and preached in a brickyard near Bristol. From then on his ministry, like Whitefield's, was to be that of the travelling evangelist, proclaiming the gospel mainly out of doors, although also in hired buildings of various kinds. For him the pattern was set for a half-century to come. Wesley became a 'missioner at large', the driving force behind a nationwide initiative in evangelism.

In reading his *Journal*, it is clear that open-air preaching quickly became the norm. Once he realized its value, he set it in the centre of his plan. It has been estimated that of 500 sermons delivered between April and December 1739, only eight were in churches!

In every generation God has his strategy for evangelism. Open-air preaching was his device for reaching the unchurched in this particular era. Whitefield was the pace-setter, but Wesley was to carry on the policy into the last decade of the century. It was his unswerving ambition to bring God's message *for* the people *to* the people wherever he could find them. He was supremely a missionary to the common man.

'Methodism's methods'

The name 'Methodist' was first coined as a nickname for the members of the Oxford Holy Club, because of the disciplined way in which they organized their lives. The title stuck, and was eventually applied to the movement from which Whitefield and the Wesleys embarked on their mission. For most of the eighteenth century it was

The preaching of the Wesleys and of Whitefield led on to a time of widespread revival in England, known as the Evangelical Awakening. Great numbers of people came together to hear the gospel, and many of them became convinced of their need to repent and turn to follow Jesus. Meetings of this kind were virtually unheard of at the time. They are now echoed in massive Christian meetings.

attached to all who were caught up in the revival.

Methodism took shape as a series of societies within the Anglican church. This form of organization was an ideal means of conserving the gains of evangelism and promoting spiritual growth. Converts were collected into classes or 'bands' within the context of a local society, and in turn became leaders, preachers and evangelists themselves. The structures of what, after Wesley's death, emerged as the Wesleyan Church were originally designed to cater for the requirements of a non-stop mission programme: the employment of laymen (and laywomen); the circuit system with its itinerant and local preachers; the stringent society rules – all these and other aspects of Wesley's sophisticated set-up were devised as aids to the spread of the gospel.

Wesley was consistently loyal to the Church of England and urged his followers not to leave it. But in pursuit of his missionary vocation to the nation as a whole, he refused to be bound by conventional notions of propriety, particularly those relating to parish boundaries. 'If a single soul falls into the abyss, whom I might have saved from the eternal flames, what excuse shall I make before God? That he did not belong to my parish? That is why I regard the whole world as my parish.'

A breath of new life

What, then, were the effects of the Methodist revival?

Its immediate impact was upon the established church which, as one historian expressed it, 'felt a divine vibration'. The initial and perhaps the determinative transformation took place among the clergy themselves. Almost all the clerical leaders of the awakening were converted subsequent to their ordination. A new breed of zealous, pioneering ministers emerged to infuse vitality and hope into a dying church.

Multitudes more, however, in all walks of life, and especially among the underprivileged, 'experienced so deep and universal a change as it had not before entered into their hearts to conceive', Wesley reported. 'The drunkard commenced sober and temperate; the whoremonger abstained from adultery and fornication; the unjust from oppression and wrong. He that had been accustomed to curse and swear for many years, now swore no more. The sluggard began to work with his hands, that he might eat his own bread. The miser learned to deal his bread to the hungry, and to cover the naked with a garment. Indeed, the whole of their life was changed: they had left off doing evil and learned to do well.'

A French historian believes that the effects of the revival supplied the 'moral cement' with which national reconstruction was made possible.

The Evangelical Awakening is normally regarded as running from 1738 (with earlier stirrings) until 1742. The years that followed saw intensive evangelism taking place, and during this longer period there were also many examples of local revivals in all corners of England.

The modern missionary movement has its roots in the eighteenth century and was a direct result of the Evangelical Awakening. The Moravians were active even in the first half of the century, but before it had run its course, other missionary societies had been formed: the Baptist, the London (interdenominational) and the Church (Anglican). A spate of organizations concerned with Christian witness 'at home' in England also materialized, including the Religious Tract Society (now incorporated into the United Society for Christian Literature), the British and Foreign Bible Society and the Sunday School movement.

Nor must the social effects of the revival be overlooked – in the areas of education, prison reform, hospital facilities, poor relief, temperance advocacy and the abolition of slavery. All in all it can be said that a breath of new life swept through both church and nation.

BACK TO THE NEW TESTAMENT

Philip McNair

The Christian movement popularly known as Plymouth Brethren had its origin in Dublin during the aftermath of the Napoleonic wars of the early nineteenth century. It sprang from two main sources. First was the growing conviction among a vigorous handful of Evangelicals that none of the established churches and un-established sects of Christendom truly represented a New Testament community. Second, there was a heightened and widespread anticipation about that Jesus Christ would soon return.

The movement quickly spread to England, and in the following fifty years to most countries of the Christian West, to India and beyond. It gained its distinguishing name (never used within the movement) in the 1830s from spectacularly successful preaching in South Devon by 'Brethren from Plymouth'. Like all denominations led by individualists of strong principles, it bore within it the seeds of its own division, and is now fragmented in many dozens of major splits and minor splinter groups. In an average town in Britain or America today there could be ten separate bodies of Christians calling themselves Brethren and all related to each other by direct descent from the Dublin pioneers.

In every sense it was a young movement. When it began, all its leaders were well under forty, and most of them under thirty. Its predominant tone was patrician; more than any other form of dissent, it attracted the 'disaffected aristocracy' and upper middle class: a typical early adherent was the Duke of Wellington's nephew.

Unfulfilled prophecy

The Brethren movement was born from the study of unfulfilled prophecy in the Bible. In 1826 – the year of its birth – there appeared an English version of an arresting work called *The Coming of Messiah in Glory and Majesty*. It was written by Manuel de Lacunza (1731–1801), a Jesuit from Chile who became a hermit in Italy and wrote under the name of Juan Josafat Ben-Ezra. It taught a futurist interpretation of the Book of Revelation, and powerfully affected Edward Irving (1792–1834), who later founded the now defunct Catholic Apostolic Church. One of Irving's disciples was Henry Drummond (1786–1860), banker and Tory Member of Parliament, at whose country seat near Guildford the Albury Park conferences on prophecy were held annually from 1826 to 1830. A participant at the last of these meetings was the saintly Theodosia, Lady Powerscourt, who was so impressed by what she saw and heard that she hosted similar conventions at Powerscourt House in County Wicklow, Ireland, from 1831 until her death in 1836.

These Powerscourt meetings became a nursery of the nascent Brethren movement and a focus for its developing ideas. But some four years before they began, a group of Christians met to break bread together in a private room in Dublin's Sackville (now O'Connell) Street: in fact there were probably three such groups forming in the city before 1829,

when all three came together at 9 Fitzwilliam Square, the house of Francis Hutchinson (1802–33), son of Sir Samuel Synge-Hutchinson, Archdeacon of Killala.

Who took the earliest lead is still debated, but it is generally agreed that the origins of the movement can be traced to the day in 1826 when a Dublin congregation of Independents refused communion to a medical student unless he joined them as a member. This was Edward Cronin (1801–82), a native of Cork and a convert from the Roman Catholic Church. 'My name having been publicly denounced from one of their pulpits', he later recalled, 'Edward Wilson, assistant secretary to the Bible Society in Sackville Street, where he resided, was constrained to protest against this step, which led ultimately to his leaving also. Thus separated, we two met for breaking bread and prayer in one of his rooms . . .' They were joined by the two Misses Drury (Cronin's cousins) and a bookseller from Grafton Street

Anthony Norris Groves, whose belief that Christians should meet together 'in all simplicity as disciples' was seminal for the beginning of the Brethren movement.

Many of the early events and influences among the Brethren were in Southern Ireland, and especially in its capital, Dublin.

J. N. Darby was the most influential of the Plymouth Brethren's early leaders. His particular strength was interpreting the meaning of the Bible.

called Tims. These five formed an original nucleus of the Brethren movement: they met in protest against the sectarianism of the organized nonconformists, and as a witness to the freedom of believers to celebrate the Lord's Supper where and when the Spirit led them.

At the same time, identical aims were crystallizing in the mind of another pioneer whose personal charm and profound spirituality graced the movement in its early years. Anthony Norris Groves (1795–1853) was a married dentist in Exeter earning £1,000 a year. Brought to living faith in Christ, he gave up his practice to become a missionary with the Church Missionary Society. To train for ordination he entered Trinity College, Dublin, in 1826. In Ireland he met other Evangelicals who (in his widow's words) 'desired to see more devotedness to Christ, and union among all the people of God'. These twin ideals inspired his life and work.

Early in 1827 he confided to a friend that 'it appeared to him from Scripture, that believers, meeting together as disciples of Christ, were free to break bread together as their Lord had admonished them; and that, in so far as the practice of the apostles could be a guide, every Lord's Day should be set aside for thus remembering the Lord's death, and obeying his parting command'. This revolutionary belief, with its emphasis on apostolic practice, lay at the heart of the Brethren movement and was acted on without delay.

Later that year, Groves withdrew from Trinity College, convinced that it was not necessary to have a university degree to realize his vocation to the mission field. When the C.M.S. told him that he could not celebrate the eucharist unless he were ordained, his conscience told him that 'ordination of any kind to preach the gospel is no requirement of Scripture'. A year later he expressed the principles and programme of the Brethren movement in a nutshell when he affirmed: 'This, I doubt not, is the mind

of God concerning us, that we should come together in all simplicity as disciples, not waiting on any pulpit or minister, but trusting that the Lord would edify us together, by ministering as he pleased and saw good from the midst of ourselves.'

In all simplicity

Coming together 'in all simplicity as disciples' was to characterize the Brethren from the outset. An intensely biblical emphasis went hand-in-hand with instinctive contempt for outward show and all ecclesiastical tradition. There was no stated ministry, but men of God were moved to speak by his Spirit. Preaching was extempore – it was the vessel, not the message, that was prepared. No building was consecrated: a barn served as well as a basilica. The Lord's table was laid with a cottage-loaf and a wine bottle complete with label. Society ladies put their rings and jewellery in the offertory. Lord Congleton (1805–83) dined with his domestic servants. George Vicesimus Wigram (1805–79) – heir to several fortunes – was not untypical when he begged visitors to his house to carry away with them any item of furniture that was not strictly necessary. Yet this simplicity of lifestyle could be deceptive, for it was wedded to an understanding of the Bible and a depth of theological teaching that were probably unparalleled in Christendom.

By 1830, when the growing house church transferred from Fitzwilliam Square to a meeting-room in Aungier Street, the Brethren numbered among them several actual and potential leaders. One of these was John Gifford Bellett (1795–1864), a barrister who wrote choice devotional works and 'talked poetry' when he preached. But first in stature towered John Nelson Darby (1800–82), the most formidable personality in the movement's history and one of the most dynamic captains of the nineteenth-century Christian Church. 'I was myself,' he once declared, 'the beginning of what the world calls Plymouth

Brethren.'

Born in Westminster of an Anglo–Irish landowning family and christened at St Margaret's on 3 March 1801, Darby was educated at Westminster School and Trinity College, Dublin, where he graduated Classical Gold Medallist in 1819. He was called to the Irish bar, but gave up a promising legal career 'lest he should sell his talents to defeat justice'. After a period of deep spiritual crisis he was ordained deacon of the established Church of Ireland in 1825 and priest the following year. It was when he was serving a curacy at Calary – not far from Powerscourt – and active in the Home Mission that a riding accident in 1827 brought him into touch with the Dublin groups.

From that moment forward, Darby's ascendancy within the movement was undoubted. More than any other leader, he stamped it with his masterful will and magnetic mind. His energy was tireless, and would carry him from continent to continent. Beginning with *Considerations on the Nature and Unity of the Church of Christ* (1828), his voluminous writings – devotional, doctrinal or polemical – influenced a wide circle of Christians beyond the Brethren, as did his later translations of the Bible into English, French and German. He excelled as an interpreter of Scripture: the prophetic system known as 'Dispensationalism' (since popularized by the Scofield Reference Bible) was largely his brain-child. His hymns enshrine the depth of his spiritual experience. When in 1830 he visited Oxford, Cambridge and Plymouth, the expansion of the Brethren movement worldwide was under way.

Winning the world

Brian Stanley

England in the 1790s was in the grip of a mixture of fear and excitement: fear, because just across the Channel in France a revolution had not only overthrown the monarchy, but seemed bent on destroying the Christian religion as well; mounting excitement, because Christians felt nonetheless that these upheavals might herald great events. Reports from France and later from Italy suggested that the days of the Roman Catholic Church – the Roman 'Babylon' to English Protestants – might be numbered. Further afield, Captain James Cook's voyages had made Englishmen aware of exotic lands scarcely known before.

In England itself, Christians were praying. Starting in 1784, first Baptists and then other nonconformists throughout the Midlands had been meeting for one hour on the first Monday of every month to pray for a revival which would lead to the spread of the gospel 'to the most distant parts of the habitable globe'. Confronted by political upheaval, widening geographical horizons and the new currents of spiritual life brought by the Evangelical Awakening, committed Christians began to suspect that God was about to do something radically new. Was the day prophesied in the Bible drawing near, the day of Christ's return? A young Northamptonshire shoemaker named William Carey believed that it was, if only God's people persevered in their new commitment to prayer and began to translate that commitment into action.

Carey had few obvious qualifications for the role he was about to fulfil. He was born in 1761 to a poor weaver in the village of Paulerspury. Largely self-educated, Carey became an apprentice shoemaker and, under the influence of a fellow apprentice, abandoned his Anglican family background to identify himself with the nonconformists. He was baptized in 1783 and two years later became the pastor of a small Baptist church, supplementing his meagre stipend with school-teaching and work as a journeyman shoemaker.

From his boyhood Carey had been a voracious reader. At about the time of his baptism he read *Captain Cook's Voyages* – 'the

Captain Cook, here seen proclaiming New South Wales a British colony in 1770, made voyages which enlarged many British people's vision of the world. William Carey read 'Captain Cook's Voyages' as a young man, and this sowed the seeds of his concern to spread the Christian faith in distant lands.

first thing that engaged my mind to think of missions', he later recalled. Above his work-bench hung a world map which he annotated with all the information he could discover regarding the different countries of the non-Christian world. The spiritual state of those countries became his preoccupation. His friend Andrew Fuller records how Carey's heart 'burned incessantly with desire for the salvation of the heathen'.

Few Christians of his day shared Carey's burning sense of responsibility for the millions who had never heard about Jesus Christ. At the fraternal meeting of the Northamptonshire Association of Baptist ministers in 1785, Carey raised for discussion the question, 'Was not the command given to the Apostles, to teach all nations, obligatory on all succeeding ministers to the end of the world, seeing that the accompanying promise was of equal extent?'

This was a novel interpretation of Jesus' command to preach the gospel to the world. Protestants had always insisted that the office of apostle had been given for the first century only, and that it was to the apostles that the Great Commission had been given. If God chose to convert the heathen, he would have to do so by conferring the same miraculous gifts which had accompanied the preaching of the gospel in the apostolic age and had died out with its passing. Carey's impertinent question therefore received a less than enthusiastic response.

Faced with such complacency, Carey began in 1788 to plan a pamphlet setting out his conviction that the commission to 'preach the gospel to every creature' was obligatory on all Christians for *all* time; it was therefore the 'bounden duty' of the church in his day to attempt to bring the message of salvation in Christ to the whole world. Even Carey's closest ministerial associates – Andrew Fuller, John Sutcliff and John Ryland – still raised objections 'on the ground of so much needing to be done at home, etc.', yet they urged him to get his pamphlet written. It eventually appeared on 12 May 1792 under the elaborate title *An Enquiry into the Obligations of Christians, to use Means for the Conversion of the Heathens: in which the religious state of the different nations of the world, the success of former undertakings, and the practicability of further undertakings, are considered.*

The key words in the title were 'Obligations' and 'Means'. If the command of Christ to preach the gospel to every creature was still binding, and if the biblical prophecies were true which spoke of God's purpose being to extend the kingdom of his Son among men, then, argued Carey, all Christians ought 'heartily to concur with God in promoting his glorious designs'.

In their praying together, Christians had begun to fulfil the first condition for the outpouring of God's Spirit. What was now required was for them to *do* something about obtaining what they were praying for. It was no good sitting back expecting some miracle of providence to transport them across the world and equip them with foreign tongues. No, those Christians who had caught the missionary vision should organize themselves into a society to send missionaries and support them in their evangelistic work.

The *Enquiry* may have convinced the intellect, but Carey needed to move

Right from the time when Carey and his friends established Serampore College, Christians have seen as part of their responsibility the education of the young in developing lands. This is not simply to educate Christian leaders for the next generation, but arises from a concern for the whole welfare of young people.

Christian hearts as well as persuade Christian minds. His opportunity came on 30 May 1792 when he was to preach to the Northamptonshire Baptist Association at Nottingham. Carey chose as his text words from Isaiah: 'Enlarge the place of thy tent, and let them stretch forth the curtains of thine habitations: spare not, lengthen thy cords, and strengthen thy stakes . . .'

Carey saw a parallel between the centuries-old plight of the exiled nation of Judah – apparently forgotten by God – and the unproductive and desolate church of his own day; in the biblical promise of a new and wider destiny for Judah lay the promise of countless new members of the Christian family to be drawn from all over the world. Once again, however, Carey insisted that God's promise was also his command. God was about to do great things by extending the kingdom of Jesus throughout the nations, and *therefore* Christians must attempt great things in taking the gospel to the world: 'Expect great things from God. Attempt great things for God.'

John Ryland found Carey's exposition so forcible that he would not have been surprised 'if all the people had lifted up their voice and wept'. Yet when it came to the business meeting the following morning nobody was willing to make a proposition. Carey seized Andrew Fuller by the hand in desperation, inquiring whether 'they were again going away without doing anything?'

That was all that was required. Before the meeting dispersed the following resolution had been recorded in the minutes: 'Resolved, that a plan be prepared against the next Ministers' meeting at Kettering, for forming a Baptist Society for propagating the Gospel among the Heathen.' The 'Particular Baptist Society for the Propagation of the Gospel amongst the Heathen' – or, the Baptist Missionary Society, as it became known – was duly formed at Kettering on 2 October 1792.

The first missionaries endured appalling hardships in even reaching the peoples among whom they were to work. Travel is still a problem in the more remote corners of the world, but light aircraft now enable missionaries, particularly in the medical field, to serve people more effectively.

The crux of all attempts to pass on the news of Jesus the Liberator has always lain in person-to-person encounters. These require that the missionary should understand and appreciate the other person's culture, and communicate in a way that culture can receive and absorb.

'So many obstacles'

William Carey landed in India at Calcutta with his wife and four children on 7 November 1793. If he had any illusions about the magnitude of his task, they were quickly dispelled. Though agreeably surprised by the readiness of the Hindus to listen to Christian preaching, Carey soon realized that the caste system – 'perhaps . . . one of the strongest chains with which the devil ever bound the children of men' – would prove a formidable obstacle to a Hindu being converted.

Discouragements accumulated rapidly. Money was short. By January 1794 Carey's wife was already exhibiting signs of the mental illness which was to last for the rest of her life, and in September of that year they lost their third son with dysentery. Carey's missionary colleague, John Thomas, took to living in grand style and fell into debt.

In 1795 Carey had his first taste of criticism from domestic supporters. Faced with an almost total absence of financial supplies from England, Carey had accepted a post as manager of an indigo factory. This provided him and his family with a regular means of support, and also money to spare to devote to missionary purposes. Some

English Baptists, however, were quick to criticize Carey for 'engaging in affairs of trade', and even his associates on the home committee dispatched a letter 'full of serious and affectionate caution'.

The pages of Carey's journal reflect his mounting sense of discouragement. 'When I first left England,' he wrote in April 1794, 'my hope of the conversion of the heathen was very strong; but among so many obstacles it would utterly die away, unless upheld by God, having nothing to cherish it.' Carey came to rely increasingly on the promises of the Bible: 'Yet this is our encouragement, the power of God is sufficient to accomplish everything which he has promised, and his promises are exceedingly great and precious respecting the conversion of the heathens.'

Carey had to wait seven years to see the promise of God come to fruition in his first converts. On 22 December 1800 at Serampore, the Danish settlement which had been the home of the mission since the previous January, four Hindus came to faith in Christ. One of them, Krishna Pal, was baptized the following Sunday; the others followed later.

William Ward, who, together with Carey and Joshua Marshman, now made up the

Organizing for mission

- *1792* Baptist Missionary Society (originally called the 'Particular Society for the Propagation of the Gospel amongst the Heathen') formed in Kettering. First society in Britain exclusively for missionary purposes. Marked beginning of greatest period of expansion witnessed by the church since apostolic times.

- *1795* London Missionary Society formed. Originally interdenominational, later became identified with Congregational churches. The society sent out 475 missionaries between 1795 and 1845, among them Robert Moffat and David Livingstone.
- *1796* First missionary society in Scotland founded in Glasgow.
- *1799* Evangelical Anglicans of the 'Clapham Sect' formed the Church Missionary Society for Africa and the East.
- *1813* Leeds District of the Methodists established a missionary society, which led to formation of national Wesleyan Methodist Missionary Society in 1818,

although John Wesley's lieutenant, Thomas Coke, had promoted missionary work among the West Indian slaves as early as 1786.
- *1824* Church of Scotland commenced its own missionary work, although Scots had already made major contribution to the early years of missionary movement, through service with other societies.

---

famous 'Serampore Trio', wrote jubilantly in his journal: 'Brother C. has waited till hope of his own success has almost expired: and after all, God has done it with perfect ease! Thus the door of faith is opened to the gentiles; Who shall shut it?' At first, few followed the example of Krishna Pal and the others, but by 1821 the missionaries had baptized a total of 1,407 converts, about half of whom were Indian nationals.

Ahead of his time

William Carey never returned to his native land. By the time of his death in 1834, the missionary movement from Britain had acquired a dynamic far greater than the impetus deriving from its original power. Yet it would be wrong to cast Carey in the role of a pioneer overtaken by the movement he initiated. Rather, he was a forerunner whose missionary vision displayed a breadth and boldness which frequently embarrassed his contemporaries and immediate successors. At the heart of that vision was the conviction that the proclamation of the gospel of Jesus Christ was the chief duty of the church and the only hope of salvation for the world.

Carey discovered from his early ventures in missionary preaching that denigrating Hinduism or Islam was counter-productive, and accordingly urged younger missionaries to 'keep as close as possible to the pure gospel of Jesus'. Victorian missionaries retained Carey's confidence in the power of a simple, evangelical gospel, but did not always heed his warnings

against adopting too negative a stance towards other religions.

Carey was convinced that the work of evangelism in India was dependent on the translation of the Bible into the major Indian languages. The translated Bible would be an evangelistic force in its own right, leading to 'the extinction of immorality and oppression, and the establishment of liberty, righteousness and peace'. As it happened, such confidence was misplaced, but it did provide the inspiration for a translating achievement which no individual has ever repeated.

In 1806 Carey published proposals for translating the Bible into all the major Oriental languages. Even Andrew Fuller was sceptical, fearful that 'by aiming at too much we may accomplish the less'. Nonetheless, Carey embarked on his grandiose project, with the assistance of Marshman and Ward. By 1826 Carey could claim primary responsibility for the translation of the entire Bible into six Oriental languages, and of parts of it into a further twenty-four languages. The Serampore translations were far from perfect, but they established the pattern for what has been one of the primary emphases of world evangelism ever since: the task of making the Bible available to everyone in their own language.

Carey's literary endeavours were not, however, confined to the Bible. 'The Trio' also devoted their energies to translating and editing of sacred Hindu literature and to the compilation of grammars and dictionaries. Carey justified this policy by appeal to the example of Paul, who was able to employ his knowledge of Greek philosophy to good evangelistic effect when preaching in Athens. Missionaries, he believed, must be equipped to meet the educated Hindus on their own ground. Marshman also commented how galling it must be for Satan to see the profits from the publication of the 'vile and destructive fables' of Hindu literature being devoted to the work of Bible translation.

But Christians in England did not share this enthusiasm: such secular projects were, in Fuller's view, 'monstrous undertakings' which diverted effort from more spiritual priorities.

The literary undertakings of the Serampore missionaries were motivated by a confidence that the spread of general knowledge throughout India would loosen the bonds of Hindu 'superstition' and thus promote the advance of the Christian gospel. Education was therefore a proper part of the missionary's work, for Hinduism had imprisoned Indian minds as well as Indian souls.

The vision of capturing the rising generation for Christ inspired the Trio to found schools, from 1800 onwards, for Indian children. Carey and his colleagues were pioneering a tradition of missionary involvement in education which has been of major significance throughout the Third World. In almost every case, such involvement originated in the same evangelistic ambition as motivated Carey.

These hopes have rarely been fulfilled; they were not fulfilled in India, and it was not long before voices both in India and in

As people of different cultures meet in open exchange around the Bible, they learn to apply its faith in their own setting. Vigorous national leaders now head the Christian churches in almost every nation.

England were dismissing educational work as futile. In the long term, missionary education in India and Africa has had a consequence which Carey could never have foreseen: the recipients of mission education have been the pioneers of Indian and African independence.

A national church

The most enduring educational achievement of the Serampore Trio was the foundation in 1818 of Serampore College. Marshman was the driving force behind the project, but all three members of the Trio shared the vision which was set out in the college prospectus: 'If the gospel stands in India, it must be by native being opposed to native in demonstrating its excellence above all other systems.'

The primary goal of the college was to train Indians to be missionaries to their own people. However, the educational opportunities of the college were open to all, whether Christian or not. Carey was impressed by how many of the leaders of the Protestant Reformation had been scholars, whose Christian learning gradually transformed the thinking of Catholic Europe.

Serampore College was intended to unleash 'the Reformation of India.' But the Trio's broad conception of a literary and scientific education founded on Christian principles found no echo in the minds of their superiors and supporters in England. English Baptists, who showed little enthusiasm for their own theological colleges, showed even less of an inclination to support a college in India which placed such emphasis on 'unspiritual' knowledge.

In terms of the exalted ideals of its founders, Serampore College was a failure. But its failure must not be allowed to overshadow the significance of Carey's motivating belief that India could be evangelized effectively only by Indians. This view was apparent in embryo in the Enquiry pamphlet of 1792, and by 1817 was fully explicit: 'India will never be turned from her idolatry to serve the true and living God', Carey wrote to John Ryland, 'unless the grace of God rest abundantly on converted Indians to qualify them for mission work, and unless, by those who care for India, these be trained for and sent into the work. In my judgement it is on native evangelists that the weight of the great work must ultimately rest.'

After the baptism of Krishna Pal in 1800,

the missionaries set out to encourage his gifts 'to the uttermost so that he may preach the Gospel to his countrymen', and Pal duly became an evangelist first in Calcutta, and then in Assam. By the date of Carey's death in 1834, the Serampore Mission had founded nineteen mission stations, manned by fifty 'missionaries', of whom only six had been sent out from Europe. Carey was deeply committed to giving responsibility to national Christians, thereby anticipating the principles of Henry Venn, Secretary of the Church Missionary Society from 1841 to 1872, who insisted that the goal of Western missions was to create national churches which were self-supporting, self-governing and self-extending.

Later in the nineteenth century, the ideals of Carey and Venn were eclipsed as missions succumbed to the influence of European colonialism and racialism. Indeed, even in Carey's own day, other missionaries criticized Serampore for relying so heavily on Indian nationals.

History has largely vindicated Carey's view: countries where the church is strongest today are generally those where national Christians were encouraged from an early date to be evangelists to their own and neighbouring peoples.

Lasting legacy

In his *Enquiry*, Carey had expressed the view that missionaries ought to take 'every opportunity' of doing good to the people to whom they were sent. Once in India, Carey was as good as his word, ready to engage in such diverse activities as translations of Hindu literature, educational work, medical care, attempts to improve agricultural methods, and political agitation for the removal of inhumane practices such as *sati* (the custom of burning widows alive on their husbands' funeral pyres). Carey's 'advanced' conception of missionary work probably contributed to the unhappy estrangement between the Serampore missionaries and the Baptist Missionary Society which marred his later years. Carey himself regarded all aspects of his work as a direct response to the command of Christ 'to endeavour by all possible methods to bring over a lost world to God'. Nothing less was required if God's purpose was to be fulfilled – to destroy evil and establish the kingdom of Jesus among men.

William Carey made many Christians of his day feel uncomfortable. His insistence on taking the Great Commission at its face value embarrassed pious men for whom obedience to the missionary call seemed ludicrous and impracticable. His independent spirit in India alarmed more timid souls in England whose understanding of missionary work bore little relation to reality. Yet he did more than any other man to awaken the conscience of Protestant Christians to the spiritual need of millions worldwide who had never heard of Jesus Christ.

That was indeed a 'great thing' for a humble Northamptonshire shoemaker to attempt. But Carey made the attempt out of his confidence in a God who can do great things. Many of the countries where the Christian church is at its strongest and most alive today are the areas which witnessed this missionary activity in the nineteenth century – proof indeed that Carey's confidence was not misplaced.

Salvation Army

Cyril Barnes

One summer evening in 1865 a tall, extremely energetic Methodist minister walked through London's East End. He stopped to listen to a group of men who were preaching outside the Blind Beggar public house. Their teaching, their methods, their fervour gripped his interest and it showed on his face. He was invited to have a word. The preachers listened spellbound.

'This is the man we want at the tent,' they agreed.

After the nightly street meetings they would adjourn to an old tent in a disused burial ground. They needed a leader more able than themselves for these indoor gatherings, and so they invited the minister, William Booth, to take charge. A few days later, on Sunday 2 July, he conducted a service out of which grew the Salvation Army.

Pawnbroker to preacher

William Booth was born in Nottingham in 1829, the son of an unsuccessful builder. He had been a pawnbroker's assistant in his native town and in Kennington, London. Since then he had been a full-time preacher for thirteen years, but that summer evening he was out of an appointment. Among the poor of Whitechapel he found his destiny.

Slowly he made converts and unintentionally built up a new Christian body. This at first he called The Christian Mission. By 1878, when the name of the organization was changed to The Salvation Army, he had eighty-eight paid helpers and operated fifty centres, from North Shields to Portsmouth as well as in Wales.

Following the alteration to the 'Army' title, William Booth became known as the General and his full-time helpers as Captains. Further military terms were introduced. A group of members became a corps, and their terms of commissioning became Articles of War. Even today a soldier, instead of paying a weekly contribution, fires a cartridge.

During the 1878 annual conference Captain Elijah Cadman jumped to his feet.

The Salvation Army began out of concern to help the most needy in the slums of nineteenth-century Britain. Now Salvationists are active in caring for people everywhere, as here among refugees who have fled from fighting in Kampuchea.

He was a colourful character, a diminutive one-time chimney sweep and boxer.

'I would like to wear a suit of clothes that would let everybody know I meant war to the teeth and salvation for the world,' he said.

Within days, Salvationists, as they were beginning to call themselves, were wearing some distinguishing mark or emblem. This soon developed into a standardized uniform.

That same year in Salisbury the Fry family of four brass instrumentalists offered to assist the local Captain in his street meetings. Some of the local toughs, who objected to the Army's way of proclaiming the gospel, did their best to hinder their efforts. The Frys thought that their playing would help with the singing and have a sobering effect on the persecutors at the same time. When William Booth heard of this, he invited the musical family to accompany him as he toured the country. The Fry family became the first Army band, soon to be followed by a resident group in Consett, County Durham. Today over 41,000 men and women follow their example.

There has never been sex discrimination in the Salvation Army. One of its earliest decisions was that 'godly women possessing the necessary gifts and qualification shall be employed as preachers . . . they shall be eligible for any office' (1870). William Booth's wife, Catherine, became one of the world's most powerful preachers, at a time when it was generally considered that a woman's place was in the home and not in public life. Their own daughter Evangeline was the Army's General from 1934 to 1939.

Neither did William Booth believe in class distinction. A farm labourer will play in a band by the side of a university lecturer, or a bank manager and a man with a title will march either side of a factory worker. There are members of parliament on Army rolls, who wear the same type of uniform as the pensioner with no other income. At the turn of the century, one Army officer was also a princess.

From the earliest days William Booth expected his followers to accept a simple form of belief, which he brought with him from his Methodist connection. The eleven short paragraphs still form the basis of Salvationist teaching. They are in line with the tenets of the main stream of the church, except that the Army does not observe the sacraments of baptism and communion.

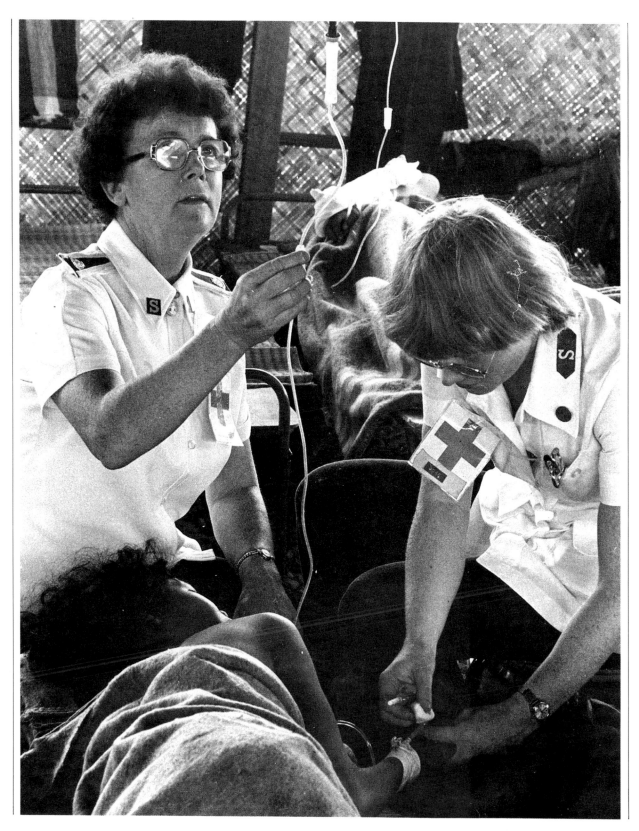

A Salvationist, even in Christian Mission days, has always been encouraged to be a fighter. As soon as a man breaks from his sinful ways he is expected to witness to his new joy.

Operations overseas

Many of the Army's early converts left the old country for lands with better prospects. They took their religion with them and soon made themselves known to their friends. In 1879 a silk worker from Coventry went to Philadelphia in the USA. He took with him his wife and sixteen-year-old daughter Eliza. The girl, although still under parental control, was already a Lieutenant and together they began to hold meetings after the pattern of the Army in England. They made converts, a congregation was built up and Eliza Shirley wrote to William Booth asking him to accept their new work as a corps of the Salvation Army. She also asked for experienced leaders. In March 1880 George Scott Railton and seven women helpers arrived in New York to make an official opening of the Salvation Army in the United States of America. Today the number of centres in the first land outside the United Kingdom has reached nearly 1,500.

Later in the year, a builder and a railway worker met in Australia. They were attending a gospel meeting in Adelaide. One of them spoke of his evangelical conversion under William Booth; the other had enjoyed the same experience. After the service they joined forces, held a meeting in a local park, gathered converts and wrote to London for officers to lead them. This request was granted and today the Army in Australia is at work in a thousand centres.

The next year (1881) the Salvation Army took its first steps toward becoming a multilingual organization when three women, all under twenty-three years of age, arrived in Paris. They had little more than a schoolgirl knowledge of the French language and less of French customs and people. The leader was William Booth's daughter Catherine. At first the pioneers were misunderstood and opposition was strong, but sheer determination and courage won through. For the first international congress in London, in 1886, France was represented by a group of uniformed Salvationists with a zeal second to none. Of one it was reported that she had previously 'carried a knife with her to stop any who should molest her in mischief'.

and had been 'a cause of frequent upsets at the Army meetings'. The report continued: 'The fierce tiger is now, by the grace of God, a lamb.'

About this time William Booth's interests began to spread into Asia. Frederick Tucker, a member of the Indian Civil Service, read of the Army's work, sent a donation to London and asked for more information. He visited England to see the Army at work, and in 1882 returned to Bombay as an officer himself with a party of pioneers. He lived to see the Army flag flying throughout the whole land as well as in Sri Lanka, Pakistan and Burma.

Far back into Indian history a child born into a 'criminal tribe' was automatically labelled a criminal, and was gradually thrown into a life of robbery and lawlessness. In 1908 the Government of India's United Province asked the Salvation Army to undertake some work of reformation. In special villages they taught the 'criminals' a better way of life and how to earn their keep. So successful was the experiment that gradually these ostracized people were integrated into society. Today the criminal tribes as such no longer exist.

Persecution

During the 1880s, while the Army was spreading round the world, Salvationists began to experience bitter persecution. Some well-meaning people did not appreciate the Army's robust form of street preaching; they preferred Sunday quietness. Because Salvationists have always been total abstainers (non-smoking was added to a soldier's commitment in 1976), public house landlords lost many a good customer when the Army came to their town. Some publicans themselves organized opposition to those who had caused their loss of trade. Then again, many young toughs took to interfering with a Salvationist's freedom of worship as a diversion from a life of boredom. Salvationists never retaliated, even in 1882 when nearly 700 were victims of brutal assault.

As in New Testament days, what was meant for evil turned into good. The soldiers' courage was tried and strengthened by all the hostility. During the worst period of persecution (1881–85) a record number of people, a quarter of a million, made public commitments to serve God.

The work of the Army became more widely known, causing many neutral people to make their own enquiries and

Salvationists are now to be found right round the world. The military command structure and uniform has proved adaptable to many different cultures.

discover the truth. The example they set under trial inspired Dr J. B. Lightfoot, Bishop of Durham. He said: 'The Salvation Army . . . whatever may be its faults, has at least recalled us to the lost ideal of the work of the church, the universal compulsion of the souls of men.'

From the earliest days the Salvation Army's purpose has been to tell people that only Jesus Christ can really change their hearts, and to make the world a better place in which to live. And this has been done not only by beating the drum, playing the music, and speaking of the love of God in the streets and in halls, but by helping to supply people's material needs.

In the Royal Albert Hall, London, during the Army's Centenary celebrations in 1965, a congregation of 7,000, including Queen Elizabeth II, heard an unalterable truth. Frederick Coutts, the Army's eighth General, declared: 'If we ourselves, for want of a better way of speaking, refer to our evangelical work and also to our social work, it is not that they are two distinct entities which could operate the one without the other. They are but two activities of the one and the same salvation which is concerned with the total redemption of man.'

As early as 1868 William Booth was providing free Sunday morning breakfasts for the poor. In 1870, on the windows of his Whitechapel hall, there were advertisements offering such hunger-breakers as Australian sheep tongues for a penny or soup for the same price.

Man and the cab horse

In 1890 Booth wrote *In Darkest England and the Way Out*. In a month it sold 50,000 copies. Reprint followed reprint and in 1970 a sixth edition appeared as a textbook for late twentieth-century social workers.

In his research the Army's Founder had discovered that a tenth of Britain's population lived below the standard of the cab horse. For the horse, when he 'falls

William Booth, founder of the Salvation Army, was moved above all by the needs of poor children, and this concern has not grown less among his followers. Here an officer cares for a young Vietnamese refugee.

down because of overwork and underfeeding . . . everything is done to help him up . . . and while he lives he has food, shelter and work . . . That, although a humble standard, is at present absolutely unattainable by millions – literally by millions – of our fellow men and women in this country'. William Booth proposed a scheme to lift men and women higher than the cab horse, and to restore them to their lost dignity.

In the development of his ideas the Army's General tackled many social problems, not only in Britain but wherever there was a need. He bought old factories and warehouses, cleaned them, warmed them and gave the destitute rest and food. Today, throughout the world there are nearly 500 hostels for homeless and transient workers, many purpose-built and fitted out to modern standards.

During the latter part of the nineteenth century many workers in the match-making industry suffered from necrosis, or phossy jaw. This disease was caused by contact with the poisonous material used for the match heads. It attacked the lips and caused incurable disfigurement. A new non-toxic substance had been discovered,

but was being used only in small quantities.

In 1891 William Booth bought a derelict factory in Old Ford, London. He fitted it with large windows and wash-basins, installed machinery and set people to work making matches – but only of the safety, non-poisonous variety. The boxes carried the banner, Lights in Darkest England. He found agents all over the country. His matches were mentioned in a sermon in Westminster Abbey. He urged people everywhere to shun poisonous matches for the sake of the workers – and gradually necrosis was wiped out.

About this time in Japan the people were becoming increasingly concerned with the horrors of prostitution, especially in the Yoshawara district of Tokyo. Christian leaders found a clause in the law of the land that allowed a girl to be freed from the brothels by making application to the police. Unfortunately, few knew of this until the young Salvation Army in Japan organized a 'blitz'.

Headed by a flag and a drum, and armed with a supply of a special Army newspaper, a group of William Booth's soldiers marched into the licensed area.

There is no mistaking a Salvation Army song. Their style of music involves brass bands, a lively beat, handclapping – and thoroughly popular melodies.

A fighter to the end

In May 1912, William Booth addressed a crowd which filled the Royal Albert Hall. He could scarcely see, his steps were uncertain, but his message was still dynamic. In what was to be his last public appearance, he gave a summary of his life's work. He ended: 'And now . . . I must say goodbye. I am going into dry dock for repairs, but the Army will not be allowed to suffer . . . by my absence.' His mind was on an eye operation he was to endure a few days later. Then the warrior spirit reasserted itself: 'While women weep, as they do now,' he shouted, 'I'll fight; while little children go hungry . . . while men go to prison . . . while there is a drunkard left, while there is a poor lost girl upon the streets, while there remains one dark soul without the light of God, I'll fight – I'll fight to the very end!'

The operation was not a success, but the warrior remained undaunted. 'I have done what I could for God and for the people with my eyes,' he told his son Bramwell. 'Now I shall do what I can for God and for the people without my eyes.'

One of William Booth's last charges, before he died on 20 August 1912, was to Bramwell, who succeeded him as General: 'The homeless children. Oh, the children! Bramwell, look after the homeless. Promise me.'

William Booth had always loved the children. He had opened Sunday Schools and had written a catechism to ensure good Christian teaching. He had provided care for the homeless and day schools in lands without government education. He had delighted to see boys playing in his bands and had taught them and the girls to be evangelists themselves.

In 1912 some people thought that the Army could not survive without William's inspiring leadership. His soldiers, now fighting in fifty-eight countries and using thirty-four languages, would falter. But the critics were wrong. Today Salvationists speak in a hundred and eleven tongues and their flags fly in eighty-six lands.

They announced clearly offers of help to all the girls who wished to leave their calling.

The drum was smashed, the flag torn, the visitors badly assaulted. But three months later, in October 1900, the emperor signed a new, strengthened ordinance which helped to stamp out this national scourge. Within twelve months 12,000 young women had accepted their freedom.

Due to the work of the Salvation Army the age of consent to sexual intercourse was raised in Britain from thirteen to sixteen. Many Christians had been concerned at the immoral practices involving young girls unprotected by law. When William Booth set to work and organized a petition of 393,000 signatures demanding an improvement in legislation, the Criminal Law Amendment Act 1885 was the result. It remains on the statute-book to this day.

In the same year, Booth decided to set up a department to search for missing persons. Ever since, every Salvation Army officer throughout the world has been an agent in this work and 10,000 lost people are reunited with their families every year.

William Booth continued at work into his old age. His very last sermon included the words: 'While women weep, as they do now, I'll fight; while little children go hungry, I'll fight; while men go to prison, in and out, in and out, as they do now, I'll fight; while there is a drunkard left, while there is a poor lost girl upon the streets, where there remains one dark soul without the light of God – I'll fight! I'll fight to the very end!'

Releasing the Spirit

Michael Harper

Over the last two or three generations, a third major force has sprung up within Christianity. The Catholic and Orthodox have traditionally formed one strand of the Christian rope, with their stress on church and sacrament. Protestants have been a second strand, highlighting personal commitment to Jesus Christ. Now the Pentecostals, though originating from within Protestantism, have come to represent a third strand. Their emphasis is that we all need a liberating personal experience of the Holy Spirit. The name 'Pentecostal' refers to the apostles' experience on the Day of Pentecost, when they began to 'speak in other tongues' in what some call a 'baptism of the Holy Spirit'.

A 1982 survey put the number of Pentecostals worldwide at around 51 million – the largest distinct category of Protestants. Add to this around 11 million Protestants and Roman Catholics who follow Pentecostal practices (see *Worldwide Renewal*), plus the African Independent Churches (see *An African Way*) – most of which are Pentecostal in style – then the figure probably exceeds the 100 million mark; by the year 2000 their numbers may well top 200 million. In Christian terms, the twentieth century could certainly be called 'the Pentecostal Century': from nil to 200 million in 100 years is prodigious growth by any standards!

Beginnings

But how did it all begin?

The traditional starting-point of the Pentecostal movement was as the clock struck twelve on 31 December 1900 – the last seconds of the nineteenth century and the first of the twentieth. The setting was Bethel Bible College in Topeka, a small town in Kansas, USA. Towards the end of 1900 the college principal, a Methodist called Charles Parham, asked his students to find out the biblical evidence of the baptism of the Holy Spirit. Just after Christmas he went to Kansas City for three days of meetings and returned on 31 December to find the college positively electric with excitement.

The students had come to the unanimous conclusion that the answer was 'speaking in tongues as the Spirit gives utterance'. Since none of them spoke in tongues they had to do something about it, so that very night they prayed for the baptism in the Holy Spirit with the evidence of speaking in tongues. At midnight a female student, Agnes Ozman, asked Charles Parham to lay hands on her. As he did so she began to speak in tongues. The Pentecostal Century had begun.

The effect of these events in Topeka was minimal at the time. By 1906 barely 1,000 people in the entire United States had received this experience. Of course, there are records of others speaking in tongues before 1900. But the significance of Topeka was that baptism in the Holy Spirit and speaking in tongues were linked together for the first time.

But in 1906 in an old Methodist church at 312 Azusa Street in a poor area of Los Angeles, the Pentecostal movement burst into prominence. The catalyst for the Azusa Street revival was the outbreak of the Welsh Revival in 1904, and the man God chose to lead the Los Angeles revival was a black minister called W. T. Seymour. When he was thrown out of another church in Los Angeles for his Pentecostal beliefs, he moved to the old building in Azusa Street. It was here that a 'weird sect' became an international movement which sixty years later was to penetrate deeply into the Roman Catholic and other mainstream churches and transform millions of their members.

An eye-witness account of the events in Los Angeles is provided by the diary of a man called Frank Bartleman. The revival lasted for about three years. During that period people came from all over the world to witness what was going on. Meetings at Azusa Street went on all night. Many thousands received their 'Pentecostal experience' and returned to their own cities and countries to share what had happened to them.

In the next few years the Pentecostal movement was to spread to every part of the world. One of those who heard about the Azusa Street revival was T. B. Barratt, a Methodist minister from Norway, who was in the USA on a fund-raising tour. Although he never visited Azusa Street, he was baptised in the Spirit in New York and returned to Europe determined to share the good news of this experience with everyone. He was to be the first pioneer of the movement in Europe and was used by God to introduce other Christian leaders into this experience – people such as Jonathan Paul (Germany), Lewi Pethrus (Sweden), A. N. Groves (India), Anna Larssen (Denmark) and Alexander Boddy (England).

It was in 1907 that Barratt visited England at the invitation of Alexander Boddy, vicar of an Anglican church in Sunderland. Soon Anglicans and others were having their Pentecostal experience, a fact which did not go unnoticed by the local press. *Strange revivalist scenes*, and *Vicar's child talks Chinese*, said the headlines. But in spite of its beginnings in the Church of England and other denominations (Lewi Pethrus was a Baptist and Barratt a Methodist), its growth was to lie within a separate stream, and it was not until the 1960s that the movement gained a significant bridgehead in these major denominations.

The Holy Spirit came on Jesus at his baptism in the form of a dove. And the dove of the Holy Spirit has become one of the most potent symbols for freedom – freedom which only God can give, the true liberty of the human spirit.

Profit and loss

It is not difficult to see why this movement grew so rapidly. It was tailor-made for the twentieth century, anticipating many of the social and psychological developments that were to take place.

Pentecostalism has always been a movement which liberates people enslaved by customs, traditions and prejudices. The later part of the century was to see the setting free of blacks in many parts of the world from their customary role of inferiority. Was it a mere accident that the first Pentecostal leader (W. J. Seymour) was a black? In 1900 women had few rights; in fact it was not until 1928 that they were permitted to vote in Britain. Was it just a coincidence that the first 'Pentecostal' was a woman (Agnes Ozman)? Today there are far more black Pentecostals than white, and women have always played a significant part in their history. In Aimee Semple McPherson, Pentecostals had a pioneer of outstanding gifts (such as dance and drama) which she exercised long before they were adopted by other churches.

Pentecostals have always stressed 'experience' rather than 'doctrine', and that has certainly slotted in with modern psychological ideas. It has proved attractive to people searching for experiences which can meet the demands of modern life rather than intellectual answers to questions. Above all in many parts of the world, particularly in the USA and Africa, Pentecostalism has become the form of Christianity most acceptable to the mass of ordinary people, nearest to their national aspirations, and most suited to be the expression of their faith. If it has not gone quite so well in the Old World, it has taken the New World by storm!

Its greatest weakness has been its tendency to divide rather than unite Christians. Pentecostalism began as a movement, not a new church, and it is still seen by many of its leaders in that light. In the early part of the century, the aspirations of most of its leaders were towards keeping it as a movement within the existing churches rather than starting a new church. But it was not long before Pentecostal churches were being formed – some as a result of persecution – and then the divisions began to take place. It was not until after the Second World War that the first World Pentecostal Conferences were

Pentecostal worship is highly spontaneous, often exuberant. Sometimes they dance together as an expression of their joy in God.

held; before that all attempts to turn the Pentecostal movement into a world church were strongly opposed, especially by the Scandinavians, whose strongest spokesman was the Swedish leader Lewi Pethrus, then pastor of the largest church in Europe – the Filadelfia Church in Stockholm.

In England the two largest Pentecostal denominations came into existence in the early 1920s. When the movement came to Wales, two of the men influenced by it were brothers – George and Stephen Jeffreys. They were to become the best-known Pentecostal evangelists in Britain (George was probably the most successful evangelist Britain has produced since John Wesley) and were the chief influence in bringing into being the Pentecostal denominations in Britain. George founded the Elim Four Square Gospel Alliance in 1926 in the hope that it would become the umbrella organization for all British Pentecostals. The plan failed, foundering on the issue of church government. The denomination is now simply known as the Elim Pentecostal Church.

It was Donald Gee who played a leading part in the setting up of the Assemblies of God denomination in Britain, which pre-dated Elim by two years. Whereas Elim adopted a centrally controlled organization (like the Methodist Church), the Assemblies of God were a federation of independent local churches (like the Congregationalists or Plymouth Brethren). Stephen, George Jeffreys' brother, was involved in establishing this other major Pentecostal denomination in Britain.

Most of the countries of the world now have Pentecostal denominations – there are literally thousands of such churches, all with their different emphases or personalities. Another influential British Pentecostal church, for example, is the Apostolic Church, which still has its headquarters where it started at Penygroes in Wales. This has a different approach to church government and particularly emphasizes the importance of prophecy in matters of guidance and leadership in the church. Apostolic churches are stronger in Scotland than in England, while in Nigeria it has become one of the largest Protestant churches. According to the Apostolics, apostles and prophets share the role of leadership, and the apostles lay hands on people for the giving of the Holy Spirit and the ordination of elders.

Pentecostals are a strong grouping among Christians in the USSR. The 'Siberian Seven', persecuted Christians who sought asylum in the American Embassy in Moscow, are members of a Russian Pentecostal church. In the USA there are hundreds of Pentecostal denominations, many of which are black. One of the few areas of church growth in Britain in recent years has been the black Pentecostal churches, though a significant part of that growth has been blacks who have become disenchanted with the denominational churches which they joined when they first emigrated to Britain.

The largest single church in the world is Pentecostal. It is situated in Seoul, Korea and is pastored by Paul Yoggi Cho (with the help of 8,000 deacons). In May 1981 it had 177,489 adult members and 12,421 home cell-groups.

The largest Pentecostal church building is in Brazil. The pastor of that church is Manoel de Melo, and he has led his church into the World Council of Churches. This is a far cry from the early days of Pentecostalism and is still rare behaviour for a Pentecostal leader, since the WCC is regarded with the utmost suspicion. Latin America has been deeply penetrated by the Pentecostal movement, and it is also the

In Pentecostalism the body is seen as important in approaching God, as well as the mind; physical posture is important alongside meaningful words. Hands are often raised to God while hymns are sung or during spontaneous prayer.

area of the world where the Roman Catholic charismatic renewal is most in evidence.

What Pentecostals believe

Pentecostals have perhaps suffered more from being ignored and misrepresented than anything else, with the result that there is still widespread ignorance about who they are and what they stand for.

In some areas of Christian teaching Pentecostals are divided. But in two areas they more or less agree. They would be unanimous that the 'gifts of the Holy Spirit', special abilities given to Christians to enrich and strengthen their corporate and individual spiritual lives, are meant to be experienced today. They all believe that Jesus still heals people, and that the Holy Spirit still speaks to people through the gift of prophecy. They believe in miracles. They believe that speaking in tongues is a genuine gift for today, and important in the life of Christian believers. They reject any view which would relegate these gifts and experiences to the apostolic age. It is this belief which has been their distinctive witness to the worldwide church.

The other area of importance is that of the baptism in the Holy Spirit. Pentecostals unanimously believe (hence their name) that Pentecost is an experience for all believers: the Day of Pentecost (when the first disciples received the Holy Spirit so dramatically, as Jesus had promised) was not a single historical event – rather it was a pattern which all Christians can learn from and experience in their own lives. The promise of this Spirit baptism is for all God's people.

However, Pentecostals do not all agree on details of teaching about the so-called baptism in the Spirit. A few regard it as actual conversion, which means that they only hold to be true Christians those who have received it. But the majority teach that it is an experience subsequent to conversion and doctrinally different. The majority of Pentecostals still hold the view that speaking in tongues is the 'initial evidence' of that baptism in the Holy Spirit. In other words – no speaking in tongues, no baptism in the Spirit. But this is by no means a unanimous view. The Elim Pentecostal Church, for example, has always kept this issue open, and does not come down on one side or the other. In Chile, 'dancing in the Spirit' is accorded a high place in spiritual experience – some even regard it as the 'initial evidence' that

someone has received the baptism in the Holy Spirit.

But whatever differences there may be between Pentecostals on these kinds of issue, they would all agree that the experience of the Holy Spirit and his power promised by Jesus Christ and received by the early church at Pentecost ought to be part of the life of every Christian, and in this they have the backing of the New Testament.

All-round appeal

Some people believe that Pentecostals are just better at 'stealing sheep' than others, and that these 'imports' from other churches largely account for the incredible growth of the Pentecostals in the twentieth century. Of course, some of their members did once belong to the historic churches. But there is good evidence to show that they have also been highly successful in pioneer evangelism, particularly in Africa and Latin America.

The reasons for this are not hard to see. For one thing, Pentecostals have always stressed evangelism and regarded it as the primary task of *all* Christians – not of just a few keen church members. They encouraged lay leadership long before it became fashionable in the historic churches.

Perhaps even more important is the fact that they have always claimed to preach 'the whole gospel'. By this they mean that they believe and preach that Jesus Christ can bring physical healing and spiritual deliverance as well as salvation from sin. Pentecostals also represent a virile form of Christianity which has proved attractive to both men and women, young and old. They have not had to wrestle much with problems of belief (the 'New Theology') or of behaviour (the 'New Morality'). They have rejected altogether teaching which has undermined the historic faith and Christian standards of morality.

It would seem clear that the Pentecostals' strong belief in the supernatural has been a powerful factor in their successes in evangelism. The healing ministry of men such as George Jeffreys, Smith Wigglesworth and Oral Roberts, and women such as Aimee Semple McPherson and Kathryn Kuhlman have drawn large crowds to evangelistic meetings. Although the proportion of sick people healed has never been high, the fact that healings have taken place and that many people have been prayed for, has been a potent reason for the success of the Pentecostal movement.

A new Pentecost

Many leaders in the historic churches have bemoaned the lack of concern about the person and activity of the Holy Spirit – he has often been neglected or even forgotten altogether. It was Pope John XXIII who coined the phrase 'a new Pentecost' in his official prayer for the Second Vatican Council. The Pentecostals have acted on the basis that the power of Pentecost is still with us. They have *done* or *experienced* what so many others have just talked or written about.

During the nineteenth century there were many revivals both in the USA and in Europe. Gradually a view developed that Christians could experience a second 'work of grace' subsequent to conversion: a baptism in the Holy Spirit. This was the view of the well-known American Presbyterian revivalist, Charles Finney, who testified to having experienced this second 'baptism'. D. L. Moody, the Billy Graham of the nineteenth century, had similar views, though because he saw his role primarily as an evangelist, he did not

enlarge too much on them. But R. A. Torrey and Andrew Murray, the most noted teachers in the next generation of evangelicals, did teach this 'second blessing', though Andrew Murray preferred to call it 'the full blessing of Pentecost' (the title of one of his books). The teaching was the basis of the original Keswick Convention Movement in the UK.

So what was original about the Pentecostals? Were they not simply continuing in the Finney–Torrey tradition?

It is important to see that where these former teachers differed from the Pentecostals was not so much in what they believed about the baptism in the Spirit, *but rather what they believed it was for*. The nineteenth-century teaching was clear: the baptism in the Spirit was to give victory over sin. The Keswick Convention has always stressed that, though they later moved away from second blessing teaching.

But Pentecostals introduced a new emphasis: the purpose of the baptism in the Spirit was 'power for service'; with the stress on speaking in tongues, there was a shift in emphasis to *worship*. Power to worship and witness to others about Jesus

Pentecostal churches in many parts of the world are full to overflowing. The growth in the Pentecostal churches, which began at the beginning of this century, has been one of the major twentieth-century Christian phenomena.

Lydia Vashchenko was one of the 'Siberian Seven', a group of Pentecostal Christians from two families in a small town in Siberia. After twenty years of official pressure not to practise their faith, they applied for permission to emigrate from the Soviet Union. This was refused, and they then took refuge in the American Embassy, staying in a small basement room for years. In 1983 they were granted permission to leave the country, and first Lydia then her family and friends have started new lives away from their homeland.

has always been the hallmark of the Pentecostal movement and its emphasis in relationship to the baptism in the Holy Spirit, rather than personal holiness and victory over sin.

There was a transitional period when Pentecostals believed in three experiences – salvation, holiness and the baptism in the Holy Spirit. Some still do – particularly churches like the Pentecostal Holiness Church in the USA. Many of the roots of this kind of church can be traced back to early Methodism and the holiness teaching of John Wesley. Gradually the holiness aspect either dropped out altogether or was given much less emphasis. This is not to say that Pentecostals are 'unholy' people! In fact they tend to hold strong moral principles, particularly in the area of sex and marriage, and have at times been quite legalistic.

A new force

It could be said that the Pentecostal churches are the first new major churches to emerge since the Reformation which owe little to the Reformation itself. English Pentecostals sometimes claim *doctrinally* to stand in the boots of the Reformation leaders. But their style of worship, their emphasis on the Holy Spirit and his gifts, their belief in the supernatural and their religious language and customs are almost totally different.

In a strange and paradoxical way, Pentecostals sometimes have a greater affinity to Roman Catholics than they do to Protestants. Both these churches (in different ways) place great importance on sacraments – they both emphasize 'signs' and believe that God makes himself known not only through the Bible, but also through signs and wonders. Catholics, for example, believe there is a miracle at the altar every Mass. The roots of Pentecostalism do stretch back into the ground covered by the Catholic Saints who often spoke of dreams, visions and spiritual experiences.

The Pentecostals are sufficiently

distanced from the Reformation to be a new church in the fullest sense of that word. Their many divisions should not detract from the importance of their emergence in the twentieth century, the significance of which has not yet been as fully recognized as it should have been by the other major Christian churches.

The Pentecostals have been called 'the Third Force in Christendom'. They have an important part to play in bringing back life to the Catholic and Protestant strands. Both of those major traditions run the risk of being 'imprisoned' – either in historic forms and practices (the Catholics) or in doctrinal chains (the Protestants) – the dead letter of the word and law rather than the living experience of the Holy Spirit. Both need to be liberated. And this is exactly what has begun to happen in what has been called 'the charismatic movement'.

The next twenty years may see the doubling in size of this 'new force'. Even if that does not happen, Pentecostalism is a force to be reckoned with already and needs to be recognized as an ally not an enemy in the task to which all Christians are committed – the spreading of the good news of new life in Jesus Christ throughout the world.

Would Agnes Ozman ever have guessed what was about to happen when she asked for hands to be laid on her? I doubt it.

An African way

Michael Harper

During 1918 a semi-literate African called Simon Kimbangu had a vision. He had been converted to Christianity through the work of British Baptist missionaries and baptized by immersion in a local river. In his vision, Kimbangu received a call from God to be a prophet and a healer. Like the Old Testament prophet, Jonah, he ran away from his vision, leaving his small home village of Nkamba in the Congo (now Zaire) and trying to find a job in Leopoldville (modern-day Kinshasa).

But in 1921 he returned to the village he had fled from and began preaching and healing the sick. In six months his following grew to over 10,000 and stretchers were piled high wherever he went. One day, he stood on a hill near his village and prophesied that a large church would be built on it, and that leaders from all over the world would come and worship there.

With the sudden growth of his following, Simon Kimbangu posed a threat to both the Belgian colonial government and the Roman Catholic Church. He was thought to be dangerously subversive. Kimbangu fled, but later gave himself up – only to be tried before a military tribunal, which was a travesty of justice. He was allowed no defence; after a flogging he was condemned to death. The Belgian king commuted the sentence to life imprisonment.

Kimbangu spent the whole of the rest of his life in prison. Deported to the other side of the country, he never saw his wife or three sons again. He died in 1951. His followers went underground. The movement he started was proscribed by the colonial administration and

The Ethiopian Orthodox Church reaches back into the earliest Christian centuries, and is African through and through. Only in this century have other authentically African churches sprung up, often in reaction to the European character of the Protestant denominations.

largely led by the prophet Kimbangu's wife. When it eventually emerged and was recognized by the government after the overthrow of the colonial administration, it numbered several million members.

In 1969 the church, now called 'Eglise de Jésus Christ sur la terre par le prophète Simon Kimbangu', applied for membership and was admitted to the World Council of Churches. On the hill of Nkamba a huge church has now been erected, and in November 1981 a party of church leaders from all over the world came there to worship with the Kimbanguists, so fulfilling the vision of sixty years before. The Kimbanguist Church now numbers over five million members and has expanded into

The African way of life has much to offer the worldwide Christian churches. There is a deeper sense of belonging together in rural Africa than anywhere else in the world. When Africans become Christians they express their corporate life in their churches, both within the international denominations and in the Independent churches.

neighbouring states such as Angola and modern Congo.

This particular church is the largest of the so-called African Independent Churches, which have sprung up throughout the continent. These churches can now claim a total of over twenty million adherents and are probably growing faster than any other churches in Africa. A recent survey has estimated that there are more than 6,000 such groups in Africa, with over 700 in Kenya alone. The African Independent Churches constitute one of the most remarkable phenomena of church growth in the twentieth century.

Home-grown religion

The key factor to understanding the emergence of these churches is undoubtedly the racial paternalism exercised by foreign missions in the period before Africans took over leadership of the mainline denominations. The local people wanted their own taboos and purification rites – not those dictated to them by Westerners.

One key issue was polygamy, a practice condemned by pre-war Western missionaries. Many of the earliest independent churches, particularly in West Africa, believed polygamy to be essentially 'African', and so practised it where it had been forbidden before. The Kimbanguist Church is exceptional in this respect – it has never permitted polygamy.

The African Independent Churches do not follow the pattern of the old European denominations. Doctrine and statements of faith are not their strong point: the Kimbanguist Church had to draw up a doctrinal statement before it could be admitted to the World Council of Churches. It is largely orthodox in its teaching on Christ and the Trinity, but still deviates from orthodox Western ways of thinking

about the Holy Spirit. It has set up its own theological seminary which is staffed largely by the Swiss Reformed Church.

Not all the African Independent Churches are pentecostal or charismatic, but the majority reflect this emphasis. Most of them practise healing and exorcism – with speaking in tongues and prophecy having an important place in their church life. The prophet or healer took the place of the old tribal witch-doctors or medicine men. The fact that Western missionaries often did not believe in divine healing and prophesying, or gave a minor role to them, meant that Africans were encouraged to join the new independent churches which catered for these needs.

The African Independent Churches have moved outside the continent of Africa. There are, for example, Kimbanguist congregations in Paris and Brussels. There are also churches in Britain among African immigrants, particularly in Birmingham. In Africa itself, there is an interesting change in attitudes: many of the Independent Churches are now looking to the oldest African churches for inspiration and leadership, particularly the Ethiopian Orthodox and Egyptian Coptic Churches.

Some have joined the World Council of Churches and this has exposed them to influences from other traditions, an experience which has been mutually beneficial. The Independent Churches have sometimes blended Christian and animistic ideas in an unhealthy way. In throwing out Western cultural baggage they may have taken on board equally unhelpful or even harmful African religious baggage.

The Christians in these essentially indigenous churches have been called 'the natural evangelists of Africa' and undoubtedly have an important continuing role to play in the future shape of the Christian church in Africa.

Christians against the Nazis

Leonore Siegele-Wenschkewitz

On the 30 January 1933 Adolf Hitler, leader of the National Socialist German Workers' Party, came to power in Germany. His aim was to mould Germany's political and community life to fit in with his own ideas. This totalitarian approach left no room for deviant views or independent organizations and institutions; the whole of public life was to be controlled or, as the fashionable term put it, 'co-ordinated' by the Nazi party. The two major churches – Lutheran and Catholic – to which almost every German belonged, were no exception to this general control.

But National Socialism also had a particular interest in the churches, and it was inevitable that conflict would arise. Nazism saw itself not just as a political party, but as a philosophy – based on extreme racism. Only the Aryan race was acceptable, and the Aryans' worst enemy was the Jewish people – hence they must be exterminated. This racism led to the infamous death camps of Auschwitz, Buchenwald, Ravensbruck . . .

Closely linked with Nazi racism was imperialism. Among Aryans, the Germans were the superior people and were therefore called to rule the world. The German people, German blood and the German fatherland were held up by the Nazis as the highest good. Known as der Führer (the leader), Adolf Hitler himself was the incarnation of the Nazi philosophy. People greeted each other with and in his name – a practice to which Christians could not conform.

Nazism was a challenge as well as a threat to the churches: it disturbed their security and forced them to ask fundamental questions: What *is* the church? What does it mean to be a Christian? What is so basic to the nature of the church and to being a Christian that it cannot under any circumstances be surrendered?

The process of discussion and exploration which gradually evolved during the Third Reich centred on three areas:
● The church began to establish itself as a separate entity, independent of the state, and to criticize the state and even actively oppose it;
● The German church became more open to the international church community, from which it received help and support;
● The church began to combat racism by involving the whole Christian community in a united struggle for human rights.

Stand up and be counted

For the anti-Nazi cause, people in Germany not only risked their lives but lost them. Two men were of particular importance in urging the church forward on its way through the Third Reich: Martin Niemöller and Dietrich Bonhoeffer.

Martin Niemöller played a major part in gathering clergy and congregations of the Lutheran church into what came to be known as the 'Confessing Church'. He was born in 1892 in Westphalia, the son of a minister whose ancestors had been farmers. In the First World War he became a U-boat commander. When the war was over, he planned to emigrate to South America, as a reaction to the Treaty of Versailles which placed the whole blame for the war on Germany's shoulders. To Niemöller, Germany seemed to be so humiliated by this that he felt he could no longer love his country or its people. However, while he was making his emigration plans, he served an apprenticeship on a farm. Here he experienced a change of heart: he resolved to stay in Germany and serve his fellow-countrymen by going into the ministry of the church.

The establishment of the Weimar Republic in 1919 was greeted by Niemöller with extreme suspicion. In this he was typical of the great majority of German Protestants. He was loyal to the Kaiser and nostalgic for the close relationship between church and state which had existed under the imperial government. When the National Socialists came to power in 1933, with the slogan 'Wipe out the shame of Versailles', Niemöller was wholly in agreement. Nazi foreign policy was greeted with great enthusiasm by the overwhelming majority of the German nation.

The Nazis also set about 'co-ordinating' the churches. As early as 1932, an organization known as the 'German Christians' had been established. This was a religious movement led by Nazi clergy whose goal was to bring the Lutheran

During the 1930s a battle raged for the soul of the German people, particularly of the young. Was it possible to join the Nazi Youth, for example, and still keep to a Christian way of life? Many tried, and only discovered in bitter disillusionment that the two were irreconcilably opposed.

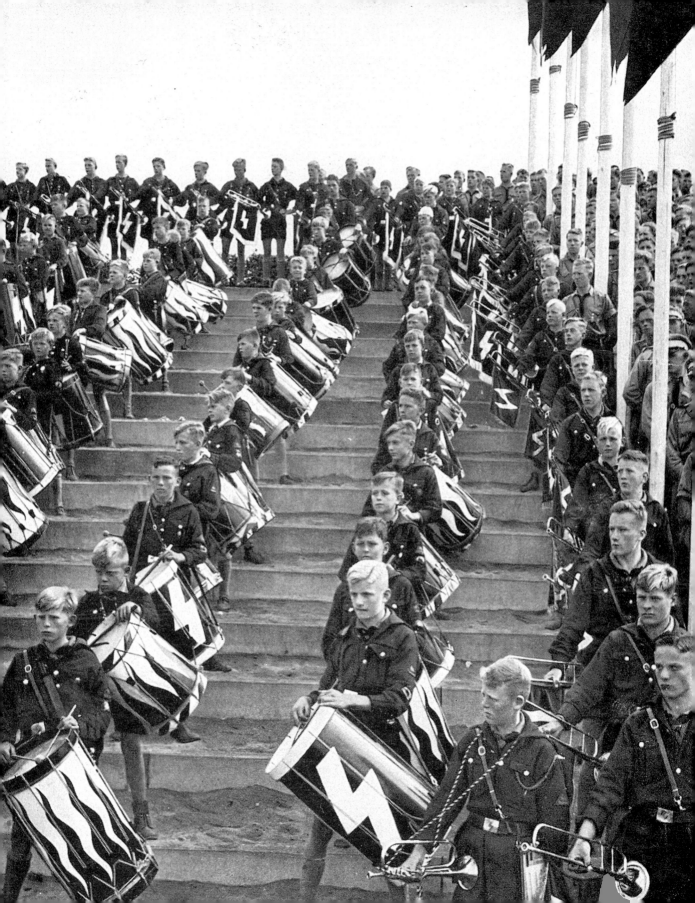

church into line with the political and ideological goals of National Socialism. In the summer of 1933, the German Christians seized power in the Lutheran church, aided by massive support from Hitler and the Nazi party. They elected a federal bishop and began to govern the church on the Führer's principles. First the twenty-eight provincial churches, which had been largely autonomous, were to be amalgamated into a single federal church under the jurisdiction of the federal bishop. Then all non-Aryans – first the clergy and then church members – were to be excluded from the German Lutheran Federal Church.

This raised a storm of indignation, and fierce opposition sprang up. Such measures were a betrayal of the gospel of Jesus Christ! The imperturbable and pragmatic Niemöller, who was a minister in the Dahlem area of Berlin, promptly organized the 'Pastors' Emergency League'. By the end of 1933 this had recruited a third of the German clergy. Congregations joined their clergy in protesting against the dictatorship of the German Christians and their betrayal of Bible and creed.

Through independent 'confessing synods', Christians in Germany attempted to establish what were the basic, inviolable principles of the church and the Christian faith. In a famous theological declaration which took its name from the meeting-place of the first 'confessing synod' in

Barmen, Wuppertal, the Swiss theologian, Karl Barth, helped to draw up a statement of fundamental principles.

A fierce battle flared up – primarily a battle between two opposing groups in the Lutheran church. The Confessing Church set its face against the German Christians and their planned 'co-ordination' of the church. 'The church must remain the church!' was the battle-cry of the Confessing Church, while the German Christians saw themselves as the 'storm-troopers of Jesus Christ'.

The provincial churches who had been brought under the rule of the German Christians were referred to by the Confessing Church as 'liquidated churches'; those led by bishops who were not associated with the German Christians such as Hanover, Württemberg and Bavaria, were 'intact' churches. Even in the 'liquidated' churches, pastors belonged to the Confessing Church and confessing congregations were formed.

But the party and the state saw the Confessing Church as a resistance organization. They attempted to destroy it by keeping its members under surveillance, imprisoning them or sending them to concentration camps. In spite of this direct persecution, many people had the courage to launch out into a relatively independent church life by applying for the 'red card' which signified membership of the Confessing Church.

The great Nazi rallies, at Nuremburg and elsewhere, symbolized a mass movement, full of national emotion and patriotic pride. It was hard for anyone to resist without appearing unpatriotic and treacherous. But some came to feel that Nazism represented a kind of folk religion that Christians had to resist in the name of their faith.

The official German Christian authorities stopped the salaries of ministers who joined the Confessing Church, and from then on they had to live on funds provided by the Confessing Church itself. Various methods of resistance were developed: censorship was flouted by a flood of underground pamphlets; laws against public assembly resulted in private meetings; censorship of the post and telephone service was made unworkable by word-of-mouth communication and a system of messengers.

This day-to-day subversion strengthened the solidarity of the members of the Confessing Church. In the novel circumstances of an underground church, outdated and traditional structures collapsed. Commitment, willingness to help and heroism were needed equally from men and women, clergy and laypeople. Important tasks often had to be taken over by women or the laity, since the activities of officials and clergy were closely watched by the police.

To begin with, the Confessing Church intended to criticize only the German Christians, not the Nazi party or the state. It wanted to stay loyal to the state, to be recognized by the state as the true church. But gradually the members of the Confessing Church were forced to recognize that National Socialism was deeply anti-Christian.

The trial of Martin Niemöller played a significant part in this realization. In 1932 a trumped-up charge of treason was pinned on Niemöller in his role as a leader of the Confessing Church, but he escaped with only a light sentence. However, immediately after the announcement of this lenient judgement, Niemöller was made a 'personal prisoner of Adolf Hitler' and spent the whole duration of the Third Reich in various concentration camps. During this period, living with people who were persecuted by the Nazis on religious, political or racial grounds, Niemöller came to abandon many traditional prejudices.

The insights he gained led to personal convictions which he declared in the public discussions on church and state after the war. For a Christian, he believed, the command 'Thou shalt not kill' is unequivocal. There is no such thing as the 'just war', especially in the age of nuclear weapons. Every human being is my brother; and an 'anti' mentality, even 'anti-Communism', has no part in Christian thinking.

Resistance, suffering and unity

As it became clearer that National Socialism and Christianity were irreconcilable, the Confessing Church was ever more ready to see itself as independent of the state. It based its life on the essential foundation of the Bible, dissociated itself as far as possible from government measures and opposed the policies of the state.

These attitudes grew directly out of the church's own experience of persecution, and indirectly out of the responses to its situation of churches in other countries. It was the Confessing Church to which other churches sought to relate in ecumenical ventures, and to which the English church (particularly Bishop George Bell of Chichester), other European and American churches offered solidarity and help.

A central figure in the Confessing Church's ecumenical involvement was Dietrich Bonhoeffer, who became a symbol of Christian resistance to the Nazis. Bonhoeffer was born in Breslau in 1906, the son of a professor of psychiatry. After university, he embarked on his career as a lecturer in theology in Berlin. In 1930–31, he spent a year studying and teaching in New York, then continued his teaching career in Germany. At the same time, he became a student pastor in Berlin and youth secretary of an international church friendship organization.

In the autumn of 1933 Bonhoeffer went to London as a visiting pastor, and became closely associated with Bishop Bell. In 1935 he returned to Germany and became the director of the 'illegal' seminary for ministers set up by the Confessing Church in Pommerania. Berlin University revoked his teaching permit in 1936; in 1937 the

Many fought in the German army without being convinced Nazis. They embodied a dilemma which always has faced Christians and always will: when, if ever, is it right to take our responsibilities as citizens of a nation to the extent of bearing arms in international wars? If we believe a particular war is wrong, do we have the courage to refuse to take part and perhaps die as a result?

Dietrich Bonhoeffer was perhaps the best-known opponent of Hitler. A leader in the German Confessing Church, he was eventually imprisoned and was executed right at the end of the war. His 'Letters from Prison' are his testament.

seminary was temporarily closed, and in 1938 Bonhoeffer was expelled from Berlin, his parental home. When the seminary was permanently closed in 1940, Bonhoeffer was forbidden to speak in public, and the following year was forbidden to write.

Bonhoeffer, however, continued his academic work; he kept up his links with the Confessing Church and also joined the political resistance movement. In 1942, through Bishop Bell, he unsuccessfully attempted to pass information to the British government about the German resistance movement. He was arrested in April 1943 for his involvement in smuggling Jews into Switzerland and was hanged by the Nazis in the last days of the war.

Dietrich Bonhoeffer collected his experiences as a Christian in Nazi Germany and reflected on them in the light of the Christian gospel. His thought and example continue to exert a wide influence in both Christian and secular circles through his writings. His prison letters, written during the last two years of his life, are perhaps the best-known of his works. He called for mature, credible Christian faith to be lived out in an increasingly secular, irreligious world. He struggled with the problem of how the biblical message of liberation and redemption can be announced to a world which has 'come of age'. The church does not live for itself – it is the church of Jesus Christ for others. He firmly believed that the good news of Jesus Christ breaks through denominational and national barriers.

Bonhoeffer himself was a pioneer of the ecumenical movement and experienced it at first hand. He deserves much of the credit for the fact that after 1945, in spite of all that the nations of Europe had suffered at the hands of the Germans, churches in other countries sought fellowship with the German churches and showed a renewed desire to co-operate with them.

The 'Jewish question'

Bonhoeffer was one of the first Christians in the Confessing Church to recognize clearly the significance of the 'Jewish question' in Nazi Germany. As early as spring 1933 he pointed out that the Jews were becoming victims of the state's policies – but his was a lone voice. He saw that the age-old policy of confrontation, which Christians had practised towards the Jews from the Church Fathers through to Luther and later, had made Christians in

Germany passive, blind and indifferent to the fate of the Jews.

Bonhoeffer wanted to awaken the church to the fact that a monstrous injustice was being done to the Jews, and that the place of Christians was alongside their persecuted Jewish brothers. He challenged Christians to regard the Jews as the 'neighbour fallen among thieves', as in Jesus' parable of the Good Samaritan. He saw that the Jewish Bible, the Old Testament, is part of the Christian Bible too; that Christians and Jews believe in the same God; that the Bible concept of 'the people of God' refers to both. But he could not persuade the Confessing Church to make a public statement on behalf of the Jews. As the Second World War progressed, the growing persecution of the Confessing Church by the Nazi authorities crippled the church's ability to help others.

Many church agencies engaged in vigorous protest against the so-called 'euthanasia measures' by which those considered 'unfit to live' were exterminated. In 1939–40, after the outbreak of war, hundreds of thousands of mentally ill, old, mentally and physically handicapped people were murdered by the Nazis. On this issue the church spoke out clearly. But on the 'Jewish question', only a few shared Bonhoeffer's insights and opinions. Only a few were able to put behind them the institutionalized anti-semitism of the Christian church. Only a few spoke up for the Jews who were deprived of their rights, humiliated, stripped of human dignity, driven out of Germany and eventually killed in their millions in the holocaust of the gas chambers.

Among these few was Bishop Wurm of Württemberg. He wrote to the government and party officials at the highest level to protest against the extermination of Jews, Poles and Russians. Against the racist ideas of National Socialism he held up the vision of a community of faith in which the command 'Thou shalt not kill' would be absolute. Against the Nazi policies of total war and genocide he held up the will of God that not one of his children should perish. So a prophetic witness, a 'call to conversion', rang out even in these dark days of Nazi Germany.

That call is just one of the legacies of the German Confessing Church which is still a challenge and an encouragement to Christians today.

Worldwide renewal

Charles E. Hummel

Recent decades have witnessed a remarkable movement throughout the Christian church. Springing up spontaneously across the full spectrum – from Protestant to Roman Catholic to Greek Orthodox – the charismatic renewal now involves millions of people on every continent.

Because it is so widespread, with different forms of teaching and practice, this renewal can be confusing. Like the reports of the three blind men on Aesop's elephant – one of whom touched the hide, another the tail, the third a tusk – it all depends on the point of contact.

The charismatic renewal is not strictly a movement like many others described in this book. It cannot be traced to one outstanding leader, or even a small group, with a well-defined set of doctrinal and organizational convictions. This renewal has sprung up from the grassroots in a wide variety of forms.

The charismatic renewal takes its name from the Greek word *charisma*, a gift. In the New Testament this gift involves all that God gives us in his grace through Jesus. But most often this word is used for a specific way the Holy Spirit shows himself within the Christian community.

The apostle Paul uses the picture of the body when he writes about spiritual gifts. Christians are members of the body; Jesus is the head. Just as parts of the human body have different functions, so Christians experience a variety of spiritual gifts. These are given by the Holy Spirit to strengthen the body of Christ in its worship, witness and service.

At the heart of the charismatic renewal stands the conviction that the full range of spiritual gifts in the New Testament is meant for the church today. This belief challenges centuries of traditional teaching that certain 'supernatural' gifts (such as prophecy, healing and speaking in tongues) were only for the first generation of Christianity.

Historically, these gifts did wane in the third and fourth centuries. In order to explain their decline, it was taught that these so-called 'supernatural' or 'extraordinary' gifts were needed only during the first century until the church was established and the New Testament was completed. The charismatic renewal replies that not only did these gifts continue into the following centuries, but nowhere does the New Testament teach that they would be withdrawn.

Paul makes no distinction between 'natural' and 'supernatural' gifts. Prophecy and service, healing and helping, tongues and administration stand side-by-side in his lists without these labels. All are

The charismatic movement is also known as the Holy Spirit Renewal movement. Its great stress is that God's Spirit can work in Christians to give them love and power they cannot find without him. Charismatic Christians often experience a sense of deep personal release.

manifestations of the Holy Spirit needed by the church in every generation to inspire its worship and give power to its mission.

Charismatic fellowship

The charismatic renewal has solid evidence that its teaching on this subject is true: all of the spiritual gifts mentioned in the New Testament are in use today. They become evident in weekly prayer and praise services. These may involve 500 people in a church or twenty in a home.

The main purpose is to worship God. Those present believe the Lord is living and personal, and as they praise him they expect the Holy Spirit to provide the gifts needed for the occasion. The members focus on Jesus Christ, the head of the Body, as they enjoy his presence and the power of the Spirit to strengthen them for their worship and witness.

Often the music of a guitar begins a hymn of worship. It might be this one, based on Isaiah's vision in the temple:

We see the Lord.
He is high and lifted up,
And his train fills the temple.
The angels cry holy,
The angels cry holy is the Lord.

Other hymns follow, many of them words

Within the charismatic movement there is a renewed concern for Christian healing. (To a lesser extent this is also true of other Christians today.) People who feel a need to be healed – physically or emotionally – will ask leaders of the church to pray for them, laying hands on them as Jesus did when he healed people. This often happens in the context of worship.

from the Bible set to music. A silence ensues after which someone may read a psalm of praise.

Another may speak about how Jesus Christ has set her free, how she reached the end of her own resources and began a new spiritual life. As she concludes many share in her joy: 'Thank you, Lord'; 'Praise God'.

The service is not planned in advance. Rather its structure develops round basic themes as members follow the leading of the Spirit. It is much like the early church meeting the apostle Paul describes, 'When you come together, everyone has a hymn, or a word of instruction, a revelation, a tongue, or an interpretation. All of these must be done for the strengthening of the church.'

One by one various members read from the Bible, or offer a prayer. They report how Jesus has given them victory over sin, a special healing, new love for neighbours, wisdom in a difficult situation or renewed joy in himself.

Once or twice there is a prophecy, a word from God speaking to a specific situation. It is not so much a prediction of the future as a practical message for the present. The prophecy may rebuke pride, call for faith, offer encouragement, condemn wrong attitudes or affirm God's love for his people. These prophecies must be in harmony with and subject to what the Holy Spirit has already revealed in the Bible.

There may also be speaking in tongues. Such a message comes in a language unknown to the people present. So after a brief silence another member gives an interpretation so that everyone can understand the message. Its meaning, just like a prophecy, is in line with the unfolding theme of the meeting. The charismatic service follows the guidelines Paul laid down in 1 Corinthians 14:27–33. Frequently someone gives extended teaching, an exposition of a Bible passage applied to everyday life.

Occasionally someone asks prayer for healing. The larger charismatic fellowships often have a special service for this at another time. Smaller groups in homes, however, where members have a better opportunity to know each other, pray for healing whenever requested. Sometimes the healing is immediate; at other times it involves a process of supporting prayer over a long period; sometimes the healing does not occur, but always the person feels loved and valued by God and by the fellowship.

These prayer and praise meetings offer an opportunity for members of the body of Christ to show a variety of spiritual gifts for building up the community, for giving new strength to its worship, witness and service. Even though the programme is unplanned, there is a dynamic movement within the fellowship as the Holy Spirit develops the theme of the meeting. People often come from a variety of churches where they are active in the more traditional forms of worship and service.

Four streams

To understand the impact of the charismatic renewal, we need some historical perspective. Although the river cannot be traced to one source, it is fed by four main streams. They do not flow in isolated channels, but merge with each other at times. Yet each has its own distinctive characteristics.

The first stream is classical Pentecostalism which began to flow in the United States shortly after 1900. (A more detailed description appears in the article *Releasing the Spirit.*) The larger Protestant denominations rejected the Pentecostal movement as another cultic wave. Nevertheless it spread overseas to Great Britain, Scandinavia, Germany and Switzerland. During the following decades it became established in Latin America, Asia and Africa. Initially, fragmented as well as isolated, Pentecostalism gradually coalesced into several major groups. In the 1940s these formed the triennial Pentecostal World Conference. Pentecostals now number 50 million and comprise the largest non-Roman Catholic communion in many countries of Europe and Latin America.

A second stream began to make its way quietly within the major Protestant denominations during the 1950s. A key person was David Du Plessis, a Pentecostal minister from South Africa, who opened lines of communication with mainstream churches. He shared the charismatic message with influential Protestant leaders in Europe and North America.

Underground rivulets formed independently at the congregational level across the United States. One suddenly splashed into the headlines through an event at St Mark's Episcopal Church in Van Nuys, California during April 1960. The rector, Dennis Bennett, stood in his pulpit and told of a new work of the Holy Spirit in the church and also in his own life. It involved a variety of spiritual gifts including speaking in tongues. The immediate strong reaction forced his resignation.

Bennett wrote a letter to his parishoners asking them not to leave the church. He affirmed the importance of their staying in the church so that the Spirit could work more freely. Bennett was invited to serve at St Luke's Episcopal Church in Seattle, Washington. There he continued to teach and encourage the exercise of spiritual gifts in the church, including healing, prophecy and speaking in tongues. His extensive travelling and writing during the following years stimulated charismatic renewal in the major Protestant denominations. Also influential in these early years were Lutheran Larry Christenson, Reformed Harald Bredesen and Episcopal Everett Fullam.

In 1963 Du Plessis, Bennett and Christenson began visits to England. As a result Michael Harper, a curate in All Souls Church, London, became involved in the charismatic renewal. He left All Souls in 1964 to set up the Fountain Trust, which for the next sixteen years pioneered renewal in Britain and influenced it around the world. The Guildford Conference in 1971 was formative for renewal in Europe and many parts of the British Commonwealth. By that year it had spread to all denominations in Britain and begun in the Roman Catholic Church.

A third charismatic current has simultaneously developed outside of mainstream Protestantism. Independent groups which shed some of the Pentecostal image appealed to many people who were disillusioned with their own churches. These groups, with such leaders as Derek Prince and Bob Mumford, have moved to a strong emphasis on community. They are currently wrestling with the whole question of church structure and what discipleship really means today. Prominent in this stream are the house churches. Many of these independent communities are linked together as informal fellowships by common teachers, conferences, cassette tapes and literature. (See *The Church at Home.*)

Roman Catholic renewal

The fourth charismatic stream began to flow within the Roman Catholic Church in the late 1960s. The way had been prepared during the preceding ten years by the Cursillo movement with its concern for a renewal in the church. Its conferences helped Christians live out effectively in the world their commitment to Jesus Christ through the power of the Holy Spirit. This movement began in Spain after World War II and came to America in 1957.

In the autumn of 1966 several laymen on the faculty of Duquesne University in Pittsburgh recognized a lack of dynamism in their Christian witness. So they began to pray that the Holy Spirit would renew them with the powerful life of the risen Lord. In mid-February, 1967, about thirty students and teachers went on a weekend conference to pray and to meditate on the first four chapters of the Acts of the Apostles. Saturday evening as they gathered in the chapel the Holy Spirit

brought something new into their lives. One professor reported, 'There was no direction as to what had to be done . . . Some praised God in new languages, others quietly wept for joy, others prayed and sang. They prayed from ten in the evening until five in the morning. Throughout the evening God dealt with each person there in a wonderful way.'

During the following weeks the fellowship group at the university grew. It began to function as more of a community using spiritual gifts to strengthen the body of Christ. This renewal spread to other universities.

In September 1967 the first annual National Catholic Pentecostal Conference was held with about 150 students, staff and

NEW DAWN IN EAST AFRICA
Michael Harper

September 1929 was an all-time 'low' for Dr Joe Church, missionary in the tiny East African state of Rwanda. The country had just experienced the most terrible famine; his fiancee was ill in Britain and he feared she would not be passed fit for service in Africa, and he had just failed his first language examination. Worn out and discouraged, he decided to take a break in Kampala, the capital of neighbouring Uganda.

Joe Church stayed with friends on Namirembe Hill and on the Sunday morning walked up to the cathedral. Outside it was an African standing by his motor-bike. His name was Simeoni Nsibambi.

'There is something missing in me and the Uganda church. Can you tell what it is?' Simeoni asked Joe.

The two men spent two days studying the Bible and praying together. In a subsequent letter home, Joe wrote, 'There can be nothing to stop a real outpouring of the Holy Spirit in Rwanda now except our own lack of sanctification.' Both

men were transformed and Joe went back to Gahini in Rwanda a new person. Immediately conversions began to take place, and Christians started to confess faults and resentments to one another. Forgiveness was experienced and broken relationships restored.

The East African Revival had started. From Rwanda, it spread to Uganda and Kenya. Its effects have been more lasting than almost any other revival in history, so that today there is hardly a single Protestant leader in East Africa who has not been touched by it in some way.

A different revival

Revivals were by no means unknown in Africa in the early part of the twentieth century. However, with very few exceptions, they led almost immediately to schism and were often linked with anti-colonial feeling. The Africans, understandably, wanted a church of their own without interference from missionaries.

The East African Revival was different from this pattern. In their 'quest for the highest', the revival leaders turned their faces resolutely against schism. Because of this, many of them had to suffer misunderstanding, disapproval and outright opposition from their colleagues. Joe Church himself had his preaching licence at one time withdrawn. Although

much later the revival movement did produce some schisms, the mainstream remained firmly within the existing church.

In East Africa at this time there was much nominal Christianity, with low moral standards and a great deal of corruption. With the rise of African nationalism, relationships between the white missionaries and the Africans were often strained. The whole situation had been exacerbated by a split in the 1920s between two Anglican missionary societies. But the East African Revival brought everywhere healing and unity, and this was one of its great achievements. Missionaries were humbled, stripped of racial pride and able to enjoy deep Christian fellowship with African leaders, who also had such a deep understanding of Jesus' reconciling death as to free them from resentment against the whites.

The revival bridged racial as well as spiritual divisions. The leadership became increasingly African, in the hands of men such as William Nagenda, Festo Kivengere (now a bishop), Yosiya Kinuka and many others. Later they were to have their martyrs in Kenya during the Mau Mau uprising, in Rwanda's tribal disturbances and most recently in Uganda. One of these, Yona Kanamuzeyi, has had his name added to the lasting roll of priests. During the following decade the movement spread to many parishes across the United States. By 1977 about one million people were active in the renewal and the annual conference had an attendance of 30,000.

In 1974 Cardinal Suenens of Belgium, an early supporter, convened a small international group of theologians and lay leaders at Malines for a study conference. They prepared a statement on theological and pastoral concerns of the charismatic renewal and its role in the life of the church. The renewal was now spreading to every major continent. Eventually its headquarters became the International Catholic Charismatic Renewal Office based in Rome. By 1983 about 15 million people

in 120 countries were being affected by this movement of the Spirit.

The streams of the charismatic renewal continue to broaden and deepen. The Pentecostal denominations around the world are growing rapidly, especially in Latin America. Within Protestant, Roman Catholic and Orthodox churches this movement is being used by God to revitalize millions of Christians for whom church membership has been mostly formal or nominal.

Like earlier revivals in the church, the charismatic renewal has brought disturbance as well as benefit. Sometimes its adherents have been over-enthusiastic and acted unwisely, so that more traditional members of the congregation

modern martyrs in St Paul's Cathedral, London.

The 'fruits' of the revival have mainly been in East Africa itself, though many Christians throughout the world have been enriched by its message and inspiration. Thousands of Africans were converted, nominal Christianity disap-

peared practically overnight, people openly acknowledged their sins and turned from them, and the church was thoroughly renewed.

The revival did not spread wider than the Protestant churches. Its teaching centred on the cleansing Jesus achieved for us when he died. But

perhaps its finest contribution has been the evangelistic zeal which has characterized it. It has played a crucial part in the expansion of the church in Africa.

Tukutendereza Yesu, omusaigwo gunaziza, they sing. 'We praise you, Jesus, your blood cleanses me.'

The exuberant singing of this college choir is typical of the East African revival. Uninhibited and happy in their faith, their style has proved highly infectious over the decades that this movement has lasted.

have been put off. At times there has been division. Yet for the most part the charismatic renewal has flowed on within the major established churches.

What marks out this renewal?

Every genuine renewal is a gift of the Holy Spirit. And renewals have certain common features: people expect God to work; worshipping God becomes central to life; new hymns are written; people radiate love towards one another; they struggle to work out their renewed life in individual and corporate terms. The charismatic renewal has all these. But it also has other marks, which together make it unprecedented in the history of the church:

• **It sprang up spontaneously.** Unplanned and unpredictable, it does not correspond to any human plan for church renewal. In an extraordinary way similar patterns of charismatic activity have appeared in widely separated places without apparent interaction between them.

• **It is worldwide in scope**, crossing most church boundaries as well as political barriers between East, West and Third World. Its basic characteristics are not fundamentally changed by differences of culture, economic system or standard of living.

• **The initiative lies with laypeople**, as is evident in the square or circular arrangement of a typical charismatic meeting. Led by the Spirit, members of the body have an opportunity to share in Bible reading, prayer, witness and using a range of spiritual gifts.

• **There is a growth in Christian community**. The renewal shows that spiritual gifts are meant primarily to strengthen the body of Christ for its worship, witness and service. This theory becomes reality with a new sense of community in this movement.

• **Charismatic fellowships expect the Holy Spirit to provide all of his gifts.** (Speaking in tongues and baptism in the Spirit receive special treatment in following sections.)

• **The renewal takes the Bible seriously as the word of God.** People develop a new thirst to read and apply its truth, and they find its authority becomes evident as they apply it in daily living.

• As people are renewed, **they develop a new concern to share the good news about Jesus.** They have confidence that they can witness effectively about him.

• **The renewal frees people to use their bodies and emotions, as well as their minds, in worship.** Praise is joyous and hearty; hands rise in worship; Christians embrace each other. There is also a recovery of the church's healing ministry in all kinds of illness including the physical.

The remarkable growth of the charismatic renewal answers to a longing many people feel. We long for a truly spiritual life, in place of a Christianity that has become intellectualized and preoccupied with techniques. We long for genuine fellowship in which each Christian finds his or her role in the body of Christ. And we long to know the power of the Spirit, in reaction against a Christianity that explains away the miraculous in the New Testament and excludes it from life.

Millions of Christians in the charismatic renewal witness to a life-changing experience. Many call it 'baptism in the Spirit'. They describe the results in different ways, but always there is a sense of spiritual freshness, a new Christian vitality. This goes along with a new appreciation for spiritual gifts, provided by the Holy Spirit to build the body of Christ and strengthen it to reach out to others. Many, although not all, start praying in tongues in their private prayers.

Yet it is easier to describe than explain baptism in the Spirit. Some link it with conversion and assurance, others with a second blessing. Many try to avoid controversy by using another term, such as 'release of the Spirit'. Unnecessary controversy can be avoided if people recognize that 'baptism in the Spirit', like many words, can have more than one meaning, depending on the context. Paul used it at least once for 'salvation', Jesus for 'service'.

When the Spirit works in dramatic and unexpected ways, the church often requires time to understand what is happening. It is possible for our experience of God to be better than our theological explanation. Nevertheless, all participants in the charismatic renewal agree that it raises a basic question: 'What is normal Christian life as Jesus intends it?'

They see the renewal as the Spirit pouring out his gifts to revive spiritual life among Christians and churches long accustomed to a level of living the New Testament would call subnormal.

Speaking in tongues

The charismatic movement is usually equated with speaking in tongues. More

than any other spiritual gift, this one causes anxiety and controversy.

Speaking in tongues was prevalent in the early church. Often it was linked with prophecy. On the Day of Pentecost, the disciples were filled with the Holy Spirit, spoke in tongues and declared the wonders of God. Luke reports other occurrences at Caesarea and Ephesus. The apostle Paul notes this gift in his various lists. He also gives explicit instructions to the church at Corinth, to regulate its use in public worship along with prophecy.

At Pentecost the tongues were recognized languages, spoken by the pilgrims who had gathered from many parts of the empire. But at Corinth the language was unknown to both the speaker and hearers; hence the need for interpretation so that the Christians could understand the message and draw strength from it. Speaking in tongues also occurs in the frenzy of some ecstatic religions. But in a Christian setting it is under the speaker's control.

Speaking in tongues sometimes comes under strong suspicion in our rationalistic culture which dislikes anything that appears irrational. In a scientific society the charge of emotionalism is the kiss of death – except in sports, love and war. But within the charismatic renewal many consider tongues to be a legitimate spiritual gift, although they do not accept the Pentecostal view that it is the initial physical evidence of baptism in the Spirit. Paul simply lists it as one of the many gifts for strengthening the body in its worship.

Most Christians involved in the charismatic renewal speak in tongues mainly in private prayer. It is a means of expressing oneself to God in non-rational speech, of praising and praying apart from the usual working of the mind. While many in the charismatic renewal start speaking in tongues in a group meeting, others begin alone in their private devotions. For some it is a highly emotional experience, perhaps like their conversion; for others it is quiet and calm like other milestones in their Christian path. Often it comes when the Holy Spirit is breaking through in a new way, with a profound sense of God's presence and a new openness to his will.

Some leaders point out that speaking in tongues is also a rebuke to our rationalistic culture. A sceptical age has turned God's good gift of the mind into an idol, accepting only what it can logically analyse and scientifically explain. So speaking in tongues can be a reminder that 'the foolishness of God is wiser than man's wisdom'.

For all its faults . . .

Like other renewals in church history, this one has its own weaknesses.

These can be an overemphasis on dramatic experiences; such gifts as prophecy and healing are more highly prized than acts of service and mercy. Again, spiritual certainty can become self-assurance, a holier-than-thou attitude toward Christians on the outside. Some people also concentrate on inward spiritual development and strengthening the Christian community to the neglect of the disadvantaged and oppressed. It is a weakness too when the charismatic renewal so emphasizes Jesus' resurrection and the Holy Spirit's power as to slip into a one-sided triumphalism – featuring only success and ignoring the cross in Christian living. The apostles learned to serve *and* suffer; they experienced the Spirit in praise and miracles, but also in persecution and martyrdom.

Sometimes established churches have been so aware of these weaknesses that they have written off the renewal entirely. Yet many churches are recognizing new opportunities in this fresh release of the Holy Spirit. They appreciate the new influx of vitality in different areas of church life. In worship there can be a fresh experience of conversation with God as he and his people speak with each other, often in creative forms of praying and singing as the Spirit provides his gifts. Individual members are more free to pour out their hearts in prayer; they become more sensitive to what God is saying through the Bible. The leaders recognize that people are more important than programmes and buildings; they are readier to hear God's guidance through the members. Pastors realize that in the last analysis it is Jesus Christ, the Great Shepherd, who is responsible for his flock. He will work through all members of his body, not just through one.

A worldwide movement

Two decades after it emerged in North America the charismatic stream continues to deepen and broaden within most sections of the church. Around the world it is now active in about 125 countries.

First in terms of size and impact is Latin

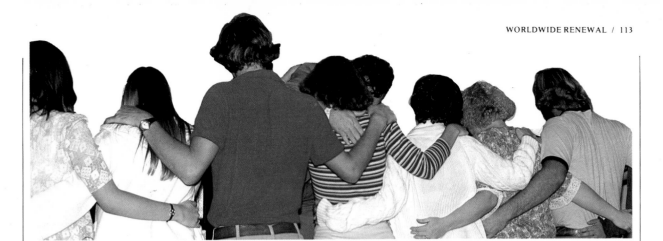

America, where virtually every country has a vital charismatic renewal. Not only are the Pentecostal churches growing rapidly but the predominant Roman Catholic church is being influenced. For example, 30,000 to 50,000 people attend charismatic conferences and national days of prayer in Costa Rica, Colombia, Venezuela and the Dominican Republic.

Second in terms of influence is North America – the United States and Canada – where the renewal began and covenant communities were born. Here the largest body of teaching and literature is being produced. Third comes Asia, including Australia. In this part of the world, compared to the masses of people, the Christian population is small. Yet among these millions the renewal is having a strong impact, especially in Sri Lanka, Korea and the Philippines.

The central and southern parts of Africa are experiencing a large-scale conversion to Christianity. A charismatic power is behind much of this explosion as the renewal is active in about 30 countries.

Finally, there is activity in all the countries of Western Europe. In Strasbourg, 'Pentecost 82' involved 20,000 people in one of the largest ecumenical gatherings Europe has seen.

The charismatic renewal seems to be entering a new stage. Initially the largest impact has been on individual lives and on developing vital Christian community in the body of Christ. While these will always be important, the renewal needs to refocus the mind of the whole church on the supernatural dimension of life. All its activities require a complete dependence on the Holy Spirit.

The charismatic renewal resembles a great river. At its source small streams race downhill with splashing and noise. At times they cast debris on to the banks. These streams converge into a river that moves with deeper and quieter power, until it flows into the sea.

This renewal will give up its distinctive identity when it fulfils its mission to bring new spiritual life to the church and to the world.

The apostle Paul taught that the gifts of the Holy Spirit are given to enable Christians to strengthen one another. The fellowship, the belonging together, in charismatic spirituality is often moving and uplifting.

Radical communities

Jeanne Hinton

The word 'radical' means a return to the roots, to what is fundamental, original, inherent, primitive. In every age there have been Christians who have wanted to return to their roots: to the fundamentals of the Christian faith, to the original Christian community, to the church as it was in the New Testament. Radical movements of this kind have often been attracted by that early Christian community and, in an attempt to recapture it, have formed their own communities.

Our age too has its radical Christian communities – possibly larger in extent and variety than at any other time in the history of the Christian church. Who do we find in them?

Usually these community people are more aware than others that they are searching for an identity, for personal and corporate significance. They sense a need to belong, to build relationships, to become whole. They want to commit themselves to a cause that offers hope – to them personally and to the world in which they

The modern community movement is often loosely structured and informal, developing from extended families.

live. Most of these communities gain their inspiration from the life and teachings of Jesus and the example of the New Testament Christians.

The early Christians

After the Day of Pentecost, these first believers 'were together and had everything in common'. They met daily in the temple, ate together in each others' homes and sold their possessions and goods to provide for the many practical and economic needs some of them had. For the disciples who had been closest to Jesus in his life and ministry, this was a natural continuation of the lifestyle they chose when they responded to Jesus' call and

followed him. They had left their homes and given up jobs to travel with him, and their needs were met from the common purse. The large numbers who joined them at Pentecost found that their decision to follow Jesus' way resulted in equally immediate and remarkable changes in their lives, not least in the redistribution of their goods and possessions.

Did these early Christians maintain this kind of community lifestyle for any length of time? There are many indications that for several centuries Christians practised a sharing of goods on a wide scale. This is apparent from some of the writings of the early church. These two examples were written at the beginning and end of the second century:

> Do not turn away from those in need, but share all things in common with your brother. Do not claim anything as your own, for if you have fellowship in the immortal, how much more in perishable things! *Didache*

> We do not think of goods as private. While in your case your inherited wealth makes all brotherhood impossible, in our case it is by our inherited wealth that we become brothers . . . We who are in communion in heart and spirit do not hold anything back from the communion of goods. Everything among us is in common, except marriage. *Tertullian*

These early Christians were also open-handed and generous to those who were not believers. They became known for their acts of charity.

The third century saw an almost continual struggle between church and state, with the Christian communities repeatedly buffeted by persecutions. But then, in 313, the Emperor Constantine was converted to the Christian faith, and a change took place in the relationships between the church and the Roman state. The empire gave full toleration to the faith.

From this time on two levels of Christian commitment began to arise. On one level, the church as an institution became increasingly identified with secular society – even to some extent the custodian of its values and traditions. On the other hand, there were those who questioned this alignment of church and state. They wanted to find once again the spontaneity of the early Christian communities and to live only by the teachings of Jesus and the apostles. For the next fourteen centuries of the church's life, this second level of commitment had one particular focus – the community ideal.

The community ideal through history

The story of which the community movements were a part has already been told in this book (see particularly *Into the desert, Return to simplicity, Life-bringers, God's left wing*). Many colourful and charismatic figures played a part in giving shape to the ideal. There is only space here for the highlights.

Third-century Antony of the Desert was followed over the next 300 years by many other 'cenobites' (people with a common life). Beginning in the deserts of Egypt, this movement spread to Italy, Gaul, Spain and along the northern coast of Africa. These men and women returned from time to time from their small desert communities to the cities, where they visited the poor and the sick, and taught their fellow Christians. There they wielded great influence among rich and poor alike.

The monastic ideal developed in more formalized ways, but in the thirteenth century Francis of Assisi turned to a different kind of discipline – that of the wandering friar. In an age when extremes of wealth and poverty sat side-by-side, he and his followers renounced all earthly possessions and took to the streets as beggars. They worked among and for the poor, and exhorted their fellow-Christians to live simple lives of service.

There were many others with similar stories: men and women such as Basil, Brigid, Benedict, Columba, Boniface and Dominic, who also founded communities. But as time went on many of these monastic communities became extremely wealthy. Some of the bigger monasteries were at the centre of large networks, and wielded great influence and power. Many of the same excesses were to be found in the religious orders as in the church at large. It was against these excesses that the Protestant Reformation of the sixteenth century was aimed.

The Protestant reformers, Luther in Germany and Calvin in Switzerland, rejected the wealth and power of monasticism as they rejected other abuses that had arisen in the Roman church. Yet still church membership remained closely linked to citizenship. In Germany, ruling princes and local councils were responsible for church appointments, so church power was in the hands of the civil authorities. In Switzerland, Calvin taught that the church should be responsible for its own appointments, but he urged strong co-operation between church and state. Alongside the Protestant Reformation, therefore, there arose another movement, the Radical Reformation. Often called the 'Anabaptists', these groups rejected the idea of a state church. They stood for religious liberty and freedom of conscience.

One emphasis of these reformers was on economic sharing. This often led to a new type of religious community, one that included married people and families in contrast to the celibacy of the religious orders. The Mennonites considered it a mark of the true church that there should be no poor among them. While both held to the ideal of sharing, the Hutterites went further than the Mennonites in establishing communities with full economic sharing and no private property.

Hounded and persecuted by both Protestants and Catholics, many who were part of this movement became refugees. Over the centuries their communities were dispersed throughout different parts of Europe, and the Americas. Initially a strong missionary movement, they also taught literacy, introduced advanced medical methods and had efficiently managed industries. By the late sixteenth century the Hutterites had founded at least a hundred communities with a membership of some 30,000. Intense persecution scattered them in the seventeenth century.

Perhaps because of the intolerance of the age in which they began, these early radical communities tended to become exclusive, anxious to conserve their original ideals and customs and opposed to change. Nevertheless, like many of the earlier monastic communities, numbers of Mennonite and Hutterite communities and congregations still exist today, and exert a considerable influence on a number of modern-day counterparts.

A feature of the next three centuries was the number of renewal movements that sprung up within mainstream Protestantism. Among these were the Pietist movement in the seventeenth century and the voluntary societies, which were part and parcel of the eighteenth-century Evangelical Awakening. As a result of the Evangelical Awakening great numbers of Christians wished to express their Christian commitment by travelling overseas to preach the gospel or by combating social ills in their own country as well as abroad.

Numbers of missionary societies were formed, many of which exist today, and also voluntary societies working for prison and factory reform and the abolition of slavery.

In many ways these voluntary societies were like some of the earlier religious communities, but they tended to emphasize the task rather than lifestyle. Because of this they were able to draw to themselves many supporters who could show their support by donating or raising funds. There was one particular weakness in this voluntary movement. The emphasis on task led to a gradual loss of a sense of community and to strained relationships in missionary and voluntary societies. It is towards a return of a relationship model that many of the community movements within our own day particularly aim.

Aftermath of war

The community scene in our own day is more widespread and vigorous than for centuries. How did this resurgence begin?

The aftermath of World War I was a time when many young people in Germany and elsewhere were asking questions about the ultimate meaning of life. A German couple, active in work among students, began to hold weekly open-house meetings in their home. Numbers soon grew to eighty or a hundred people. The young people who came were largely from Christian groups, but also anarchists, atheists, artists and others.

Some years previously Eberhard and Emmy Arnold had studied some old Anabaptist writings and had been greatly stirred by what they read. Now in these open-house meetings they began to study the Sermon on the Mount and the stories about the days after Pentecost. Here they saw the answer to their seeking and questioning: community of faith, love and goods. This led to the founding of the Hutterian Society of Brothers, with its first 'Bruderhof' (primitive church-community) at Sannerz, a small village in Germany.

That first community numbered just seven. They ran a publishing house and a small farm, and offered hospitality to numerous guests. They aimed at simplicity and poverty for the sake of Jesus, and their common life attracted many others (young people and families) who came to join

Everyone experiences from time to time a friendship and a closeness over a meal together. Meal times are particularly significant in community living, as old and young meet together simply and without barriers.

them. They stood out against Hitler and refused to take part in World War II, so they had to leave Germany. They fled first to England and later to Paraguay, until in 1954 they emigrated to the United States. There are now three communities in the USA and one in England. They support themselves by publishing and making toys and each Bruderhof has its own school up to secondary-school age or eighth grade.

Understandably, many of the communities that arose in the immediate post-war periods have been strong on unity between people and peace between nations. One of the best known is Taizé, an ecumenical community in Burgundy, France. In recent years, it has become a place of pilgrimage for thousands of young people, who camp nearby and share for short periods of time in the life and worship of the community.

In the summer of 1940, several months after the outbreak of World War II and with France already defeated by the German forces, an idea began to grow in the mind of a young Swiss theological student, Roger

THE CHURCH AT HOME
Charles E. Hummel

The modern house church movement has both captured allegiance and caused anxiety.

Many acclaim it as a rediscovery of New Testament Christianity, while others see in it an escape from the realities of established church life.

The early Christian community started as a house church. The record in the book of Acts tells us that 'They devoted themselves to the apostles' teaching and to the fellowship . . . They broke bread in their homes and ate together with glad and sincere hearts.' Some twenty-five years later, the apostle Paul wrote to friends in Rome: 'Greet also the church that meets in their house.'

During the following decades the Christians continued to meet in homes. In times of persecution they went underground into the catacombs. But after the Roman Emperor Constantine legalized Christianity in AD 313, church buildings began to multiply. In

Schutz. Later he was to write that 'the defeat of France awoke powerful sympathy. If a house could be found there, of the kind we had dreamed of, it would offer a possible way of assisting some of those most discouraged, those deprived of a livelihood; and it could become a place of silence and work . . .'

Roger Schutz's mother was French, his father Swiss. At thirteen he left home to attend a secondary school some distance away, lodging with a Catholic family. These early years shaped his ecumenical vision. While the Germans were still occupying France, Roger Schutz bought a house in Taizé and opened it to refugees, many of them Jews. He chose the village because it was poor and isolated, and his father had always taught him that Jesus is closest to the poor. It was not long before his activities became known and the house was taken over by the Gestapo. He had to flee to Switzerland, but he returned to reopen the house in 1944. Others joined him to form the Community of Taizé.

the sixteenth and early seventeenth centuries, the Reformation fostered new churches as Protestants built their own places of worship. Yet in every century Christians have met in homes in small groups to supplement their more formal church life.

Others, however, have left the established denominations to form independent house churches. It is this latter development, evident since the mid-twentieth century, that can be called 'the house church movement'.

The same but different

The thousands of house churches around the world vary widely in origin and purpose.

In England three main branches have originated independently of each other as offshoots of established denominations. They have no central organization and want to be known simply as local churches. Yet each 'chain' of house churches has a distinctive character. They are linked by the itinerant ministry of their leaders, common hymns and conferences, similar behaviour patterns and visits among the 'member' churches. They now number several hundred with about 50,000 members.

In the United States a similar movement in the last two decades has been nurtured by the charismatic renewal (see *Worldwide renewal*). While most of the participants in this renewal have remained in the Roman Catholic and mainstream Protestant churches, many have left them to form small informal house churches. Their rapid growth is due also to winning new converts from non-religious backgrounds. The various chains have the common linking features noted above as well as teaching on cassette tapes, in magazines and in books. Members number several hundred thousand.

The house church movement has also developed in Latin America and certain Communist countries. The largest has appeared in China, as the government outlawed Christianity and confiscated buildings. These churches are completely indigenous, unconnected with any outside organizations. They rely on lay leadership, since churches are not allowed to support full-time workers. Leaders usually emerge when the groups meet together for prayer; they are recognized and appointed by members of the church. Evangelism takes place through personal contact with friends and neighbours. The Chinese house churches are fully self-governing, self-supporting and self-propogating. Flexible and adaptable to local needs, they enabled Christianity to survive and even prosper through the dark days of the Cultural Revolution. Membership today is numbered in the millions.

Amid the wide diversity of environment, origin and activities, these house churches have much in common:
● Strong, supportive personal relationships and a concern to express in practical ways the apostle Paul's teaching about Christians being 'members of the Body of Christ';
● Flexibility and spontaneity in worship and prayer in the context of the home;
● Intensive biblical instruction of new members and children;
● Mutual strengthening of the members, including sharing of material goods as in the early church;
● Investment of money and time in people rather than expensive buildings. Large meetings are held on occasion in rented buildings.

All this shows how strong and vital this movement is. Yet its very freedom and flexibility make it susceptible to isolation, divisions and cultic trends led by false prophets. Some house churches demand a total commitment of the members' time and energy, often concentrating on the community's own concerns to the neglect of the wider work of God in the world.

Eventually many of these house churches will face the problems of over-organization and rigidity encountered by the established churches. The test of this growing movement will be the success of 'second generation' members – those who have grown up within it – in dealing with these problems and persevering in the 'apostles' teaching' as set out in the Bible.

The members of the community work in parishes or have secular jobs. They aim to permeate society with their vision of peace and unity. The brotherhood is pledged to work for Christian unity, particularly among the Catholic and Reformed churches.

Another community that had its beginnings in the post-war years is the Evangelical Sisterhood of Mary in Darmstadt, Germany. Its two founders, Mary Schlink and Erika Maddaus, are the two 'mothers' of the community. The sisterhood began as a small Bible study group and later grew into a religious community. Those who gathered together to study the Bible in the early days were deeply convicted of the sins of their nation, which had led to World War II and to the persecution of the Jews. This has given the community its emphasis on daily repentance from sin, alongside prayer, Bible teaching and evangelism. Like Taizé, the sisterhood attracts many thousands of visitors, who have been influenced by the example and witness of the community. Daughter houses have been established in Israel, England and the USA and at Darmstadt there is also now a small

brotherhood associated with the sisterhood.

Rediscovering a purpose

In Britain, one effect of the war was to expose a spiritually poor nation and an irrelevant church. Army chaplains discovered how few of their men had any real understanding of the Christian message. For the first time a religious opinion poll was taken and its finding caused widespread concern. In 1943, William Temple, the Archbishop of Canterbury, called together a commission to 'survey the whole problem of modern evangelism'. The aim was to prepare the Church of England for concerted action once the war was ended. A report *Towards the Conversion of England* was published in 1944; in particular, it highlighted the need to mobilize and train laypeople for evangelism.

At the same time as this report was being compiled, an Anglican clergyman, Roger de Pemberton (himself a member of the commission) was energetically working on an idea of his own. Before the outbreak of war, he had begun to run holiday houseparties, renting private schools for this purpose during the holiday seasons. These houseparties offered a programme of holiday activities with an epilogue each evening, and they proved an immediate success. In the easy, informal atmosphere, many nominal Christians found a living faith for the first time; others rediscovered a purpose for their Christian lives. A week or a fortnight spent in the company of a large number of other Christian people proved in itself a powerful influence – an experience of Christian community.

With his thinking stimulated further by the work of the commission on evangelism, Roger de Pemberton began to think about setting up a permanent centre, run by a resident Christian community. The place he had in mind was Lee Abbey in Devon, formerly a manor house, at that time a private school. Others caught his enthusiasm for the idea, and despite the daunting task in the post-war years of raising money to buy and restore the house, Lee Abbey was opened in 1945 as a 'centre for evangelism within the Church of England'.

Another similar centre, a sister-community, Scargill, was opened in the north of England. These are centres to which people from all walks of life come for holidays and conferences and where in relaxed surroundings they are stimulated to think about the renewal of faith and witness in the modern age. Many of the suggestions of the original report *Towards the Conversion of England* were considered too revolutionary and never taken up, but they have been and continue to be embodied in the life and work of these communities and others like them, which have sprung up in the intervening years.

Community and the youth culture

The 50s were years when disenchanted young people were beginning to voice their impatience with the values and lifestyle of Western, consumer-oriented society. Many gathered in parts of Europe and Asia, took to drugs and made their protest known by dropping out of society. Some found their way to the Swiss chalet home of an American professor, Francis Schaeffer, and his wife, Edith. There they found a welcome, a sympathetic hearing and answers that made sense to them both intellectually and emotionally.

Like the young people who found their way to the Arnolds' home in Germany in the 1930s, these young people were encouraged to study the Bible and to trust in a God who answers prayer. Such answers to prayer were many, as God provided for the many material and financial needs of a growing fellowship at the Schaeffers' home in Huémoz, Switzerland. Soon the Schaeffers' chalet was linked to others nearby and the L'Abri Fellowship was formed (L'Abri means 'the shelter'.) The fellowship served a continuous stream of guests, many from ordinary walks of life as well as hippies and drop-outs. Ancillary houses were soon established in England, Holland, Italy and France.

The Shalom covenant

The 60s and 70s saw an even more rapid growth in the community movement, with numbers of Christian communities emerging from the charismatic renewal and the evangelical awakenings of these years, from the social concerns of their founders and from recently-established missionary movements. Several of these communities also have roots in the Anabaptist tradition and therefore acknowledge a debt to their Mennonite and Hutterite forebears. Many of these communities have established or are establishing wide networks, as communities with similar concerns and lifestyles link up and associate with one another, nationally and internationally.

One community influenced by Anabaptist concepts is Reba Place Fellowship, in the USA. Some students at Goshen College in Indiana were studying the sixteenth century 'radical reformation', which had given birth to such groups as the Hutterite and Mennonite communities. They began to wonder what would happen if they began to take seriously the same concepts of brotherhood and sharing and apply them to life in twentieth-century America.

Three of these students bought a house called Reba Place on a small street in Evanston, Illinois, and from there the group began to grow. In the 60s the community grew to 140 adults and children housed in twelve buildings, all within walking distance of each other. Others lived in rented apartments nearby. Most of the working members of the fellowship held jobs as teachers, blue-collar workers, social workers and psychologists. They put all their income into a common purse, from which all personal and family living allowances were distributed. They felt called to be a

Ever since the days of the first monasteries, simple, everyday tasks have formed an important part of community life, and they still do. This is partly from necessity, of course, and partly because these jobs are a great leveller. But they are also a deliberate attempt to rediscover the simplicity and naturalness modern society has lost.

church, a radical example of love and sharing at the heart of society. Their influence on their immediate neighbourhood was considerable, transforming a racially divided neighbourhood into one that was stable and integrated.

In more recent years Reba Place has drawn a number of other communities into a covenant relationship with itself to form the 'Shalom Covenant', committed to a life based on Jesus' radical teaching, each community encouraging and helping the others, each seeing itself as the church in its own locality.

Community of communities

The late 60s and 70s were years of charismatic renewal (see *A worldwide renewal*). This movement, with its emphasis on spontaneity and warmth, soon began to express these in a community lifestyle.

In the episcopal church in the USA, the story of the Church of the Redeemer, Houston, attracted considerable publicity. Its rector, Graham Pulkingham, moved to the church in 1963. It was a dying church in a poor neighbourhood, yet Graham longed to build an effective neighbourhood church that genuinely served the people who lived around it. But he soon realized how powerless he was to offer anything effective to the many poor people, Latins and blacks.

Graham grew disillusioned and discouraged but this led to a deep searching. Finally he came to a new experience of being inwardly filled by the Holy Spirit. His own life and ministry were transformed, and so was the church. The Christians experienced a strong sense of God's presence and power in worship, and they began to use gifts of the Spirit, including prophecy, speaking in tongues and gifts of healing. There was a new emphasis on prayer and Bible study. In particular, those who were drawn to the church, both from the neighbourhood and further afield, began to feel a deep love for one another and a new desire to serve the many troubled people around them. Some, including Graham Pulkingham and his family, opened their homes to those in need and began to 'slip into community living, almost without knowing it'.

Within a comparatively short time numbers had grown from a small handful to a church community of 400, with some fifty community households ministering to different needs and contributing to the sharing of gifts and resources. In 1973 Graham Pulkingham was invited by the Bishop of Coventry to travel to England and share with the church in Britain his vision of community ministry.

In Britain, something similar was happening in a small village in Dorset, also as a result of the charismatic renewal. A titled couple, Sir Tom and Lady Faith Lees, had read a book about evangelism in gangland New York (Dave Wilkerson's *The Cross and the Switchblade*). This had led them to seek for themselves a baptism in the Holy Spirit. As a result, they found God's power at work in new ways, and the small Bible study group that met in their home grew from a dozen to some 200 people coming weekly for teaching and prayer. People were converted, filled with the

Spirit and healed. Tom and Faith Lees, together with a small team drawn mainly from local churches, began to run camps and conferences centred on their home, Post Green. They also drew into their family a number of people who needed emotional healing, and as happened in Houston this soon led to others similarly opening their homes. A genuine community had been born.

When the Pulkinghams came to England and established the Community of Celebration (now on the Isle of Cumbrae, Scotland, and in Colorado, USA), they formed links with Post Green. A friendship resulted which led to growing co-operation and sharing of resources. These communities work for the renewal of church and society. In particular, they help local churches to develop ways of living and relating together which are appropriate to their own circumstances.

Friendships thus established have caused a number of communities to come together and form supportive networks, which enable them to share and to learn from one another. The Communities of Celebration in the USA and the UK, Post Green Community in the UK and Sojourners' Fellowship in Washington D.C. have thus come together with a number of other communities to form 'a community of communities'. (Sojourners are a church-community which grew out of the activities of a group of young evangelical Christians, concerned to see gospel principles applied to social and political issues.)

In a Christian community, whether living together or simply coming from their separate homes to meet together, each person matters to the others, as part of the whole. Believing that we all matter to God, Christians learn to accept one another without reserve. This is a vital part of human freedom.

Base communities

Another strong community movement is exerting a considerable influence in Latin America, Africa and Asia and is beginning to grow in Europe. This is the 'base community' movement within the Roman Catholic Church.

Originally a spontaneous movement among Roman Catholics in underdeveloped countries, the base communities gained a new impetus and direction as a result of the Second Vatican Council's recognition and encouragement. They are really more of a cell movement within the Roman Catholic Church than a deliberate search for a community lifestyle. The countries in which they have flourished are those where people still live as local or rural communities, but where there is considerable poverty and oppression. They thus have brought people together around a common faith and a common cause. Their own belief is in Jesus' concern for the poor and oppressed in society. They have therefore become a social and political movement as well as a religious movement.

In search of distinctively Christian lives

Each of these communities and networks constitutes a force for renewal within both church and society. There are tensions in their relationship with the institutional church, as there have been throughout Christian history. Yet they have a vital part to play – they remind the traditional churches that they are called to keep alive in the world the lifestyle and the mission of Jesus.

These communities have been and are mostly fringe movements within the Christian church, and so they are bound to be vulnerable to false teachings, to extreme and even dubious practices, to a dangerous authoritarianism and to utopian and perfectionist values. But the mainstream denominations stand constantly in an equally severe danger of comfortably conforming to the status quo and being locked in outmoded traditions and practices. Both groups need each other, and they have served each other throughout history in this way, certainly since the era of Constantine.

Yet perhaps something is taking place in our own day. The divisions between church and para-church structures may be breaking down. The process of secularization has reached a point where the Christian church must return to the stance it took before the Emperor Constantine brought it under the state's wing. The divisions between church and society must become more closely marked once more.

All this means that a distinctive Christian lifestyle is becoming incumbent on all Christians, not just on a few who feel specially called to it. The growing Christian radical community movement is spearheading the way. It will probably continue to take that place at one end of the spectrum. But there are many who long that increasingly we are going to see the whole church finding again what it means to be a radical Christian community.